Critical analysis of the plot elements of the novel Digital Fortress
Between fiction and reality

Dougglas Hurtado Carmona
Yesenia Vidal Martínez
Gustavo Adolfo Matos
Evelyn Muñiz Pérez

Critical analysis of the plot elements of the novel Digital Fortress

Between fiction and reality

Critical analysis of the plot elements of the novel Digital Fortress Between fiction and reality

Douglas Hurtado Carmona
Yesenia Vidal Martínez
Gustavo Adolfo Matos
Evelyn Muñiz Pérez

ISBN (Print): 978-1-312-52300-5
ISBN (Epub): 978-1-312-52298-5
©Copyright 2023.
First edition

Contact: dougglas@gmail.com

Translate from Análisis crítico de los elementos de la trama de la Nnovela La Fortaleza Digital

Front page:
Adapted from Hacker using laptop with cyber security lettering on screen near computer monitors on black depositphotos # 342534240 © VitalikRadko

No part of this publication, including its cover design and illustrations, may be reproduced, stored or transmitted in any form or by any means of any kind without prior permission from the publisher.

SCIENTIFIC COMITTEE

Luis Armando Cobo Campo
PhD. in Computer Engineering from the University of Montreal, Canada, PhD in Engineering from the Universidad de los Andes. Master in Systems and Computing Engineering, Systems and Computing Engineer, Universidad de los Andes. Dean Faculty of Systems Engineering. With more than 15 years of experience in teaching and research in the areas of computer programming, embedded systems, new programming paradigms, artificial intelligence and computer networks.

Francis Araque Barboza
PhD in Human Sciences, Master in Public Management, Sociologist (Universidad del Zulia, Venezuela). Researcher, postgraduate and doctoral professor, University of Zulia. National Experimental University Rafael María Baralt. More than 36 years of professional experience. Publication of articles. Tutor for master's and doctoral theses. International speaker. Professor at the undergraduate, postgraduate and Doctorate levels, Principal Investigator and co-investigator of Research Projects, 30 years of experience in Teaching and research in Higher Education, member of the EDUSAR research group, thesis tutor at the undergraduate, postgraduate and Doctorate levels, family area, disability, gender, identities, intrafamily abuse. Deepening in the area of philosophy, epistemology and qualitative research.

Jorge Luis Vengoechea Orozco
PhD in Innovation Management. Master of Business Administration University of Louisville. Professor and researcher at the Metropolitan University of Barranquilla. Academic Advisor. He was dean of the Faculty of Economic and Administrative Sciences

CONTENT

INTRODUCTION 1

DIGITAL FORTRESS 3

    Digital Fortress book... 4
    Dan Brown as Author 5
    Contributions of the book 6

PLOT ELEMENTS WITH BIAS TOWARDS REALITY 7

    Kanji 8
    1980s and email.. 9
    Cryptography 11
    three million processors 13
    Transltr capacity 14
    A mathematical impossibility 15
    brute force attack 17
    self-encryption.. 18
    Send emails to a dead account 20
    Spain is not the capital of cryptography 21
    automobile with gagets 23
    Single public key encryption standard.. 24
    Telephone number length 27
    LIMBO language was based on C and Pascal 28
    Sys-Sec 29
    TRANSLTR Power Consumption... 31
    Calculated immediate of the probabilities 32

FICTIONAL PLOT ELEMENTS 35

    Intelligence quotient 35
    substitution cipher 37
    transltr the supercomputer 38
    In 1990, access codes had more than 50 characters................................. 40
    Investment in the NSA 42
    Bergofsky's principle.. 43
    Encryption algorithms, mathematical formulas 45
    NDAKOTA@ara.anon.org 47
    Tracker... 48
    LIMBO language tracker 50
    ARA forward the emails you receive 51

- Brainstorm Software 53
- Software to shape complex strategies and predict weak points 54
- Backdoor hidden in the algorithm 56
- Monocle 58
- miniature computer 59
- Monocle Features 60
- Transltr decrypt a file in three hours 62
- Mitten is the best 63
- Transltr always works with its freon cooling system 64
- non-conformist search 65
- Diverter Switch in Mitten 67
- In TRANSLTR the virus has blocked the processors 68
- mutation chains 69
- The brainstorming sessions 71
- Dangerous chains of mutation 72
- viruses reproduce 73
- Welcome to digital extortion 76

CONCLUSIONS 79

BIBLIOGRAPHY 83

Introduction

Dan Brown's "Digital Fortress" oscillates between fact and fiction, creating a highly technological and fascinating world that captures the reader's imagination. After a detailed analysis of various plot elements in the novel, both real and fictional tendencies that contribute to the overall plot and appeal of the story can be identified.

Examining the reality-leaning elements, we find that Brown makes effective use of his research and technological savvy to give his plot a sense of authenticity. He uses authentic writing systems like Kanji, accurately portrays the development of technologies like email, and shows a strong understanding of cryptography and its importance in information security. However, he sometimes tends to exaggerate certain aspects, such as the capacity and sophistication of supercomputers, which is still beyond our current technological capabilities.

On the other hand, fictionalized plot elements such as TRANSLTR the supercomputer, Bergofsky's principle, and constantly reproducing computer viruses add a touch of emotion and drama to the story. Although these elements are somewhat based on reality, they are exaggerated or idealized to meet the needs of the plot and keep readers engaged.

Through the deft blend of real and fictional elements, Brown has created in "Digital Fortress" a highly technological parallel world that feels intriguingly possible. Although some plot elements may be unrealistic from a technical or scientific perspective, they serve their purpose of keeping the plot moving and engaging the reader.

In addition, beyond entertainment, "Digital Fortress" raises important reflections on privacy, security and the role of technology in our society. In this sense, although the book leans more towards fiction than reality, it remains relevant and intriguing, and invites us to question our reality and reflect on these crucial issues.

The analysis described in this book is divided into two sections.

In the first section, the elements of the plot that tend towards reality will be examined. This includes things like the "Kanji" writing system, the "1980s and email," and fundamental cryptography concepts like "brute force attack" and "self-encryption." Although these elements are based on true events and precise technical concepts, the ways in which Brown has adapted them for his novel will also be discussed.

The second section focuses on plot elements that tend towards fiction. This includes concepts like "Transltr the supercomputer", the "Bergofsky Principle", and the intriguing "Tracer". Although these elements are based on fiction, the ways in which Brown has infused them with a touch of reality to give his plot a sense of authenticity will be discussed.

Through this analysis, Brown's ability to balance fact and fiction in his novel, using both elements to create a plot that is both captivating and plausible, will be revealed. It will also be shown how Brown uses his technical knowledge and attention to detail to add depth to her narrative and keep readers on their toes until the very last page.

Digital Fortress

In the book "Digital Fortress" by Dan Brown, the concept of a digital fortress is introduced as an advanced computer security infrastructure used to protect critical data and systems. Although the novel is a work of fiction, we can analyze the concept of digital fortress from a critical perspective and explore its relationship with the reality of computer security.

A digital fortress can be understood as a set of measures and technologies designed to safeguard information and prevent unauthorized access. It is characterized by the implementation of authentication mechanisms, data encryption, intrusion detection and security management systems.

According to a study by Smith and Johnson (2018), a digital fortress is built on the basis of a layered security architecture, where different levels of protection overlap to form a strong defensive barrier. This defense-in-depth strategy involves combining physical, technical, and administrative controls to mitigate risk and protect digital assets.

In practice, a digital fortress can include firewalls, intrusion detection and prevention systems, log monitoring, multi-factor authentication, data encryption, and strong security policies (Anderson et al., 2020). These measures are essential to ensure the confidentiality, integrity and availability of information in digital environments.

It is important to note that while the concept of a digital fortress presents valuable insights into computer security, the representation in the book may overstate the effectiveness and complexity of digital fortresses. In the real world, computer security is an ever-evolving challenge, and there is no such thing as a completely foolproof protection system.

A digital fortress is a concept that encompasses the measures and technologies implemented to protect information and systems in the field of computer security. Although Dan Brown's book provides a fictitious view of these strengths, it serves as a starting point to reflect on the importance of digital security and the need to implement adequate protection strategies.

Digital Fortress book

"Digital Fortress" is a novel written by Dan Brown that combines elements of technology, intrigue and suspense to create a story full of twists and emotions. Published in 1998, the book presents a plot in which the National Security Agency (NSA) confronts a computer threat that puts national security at risk.

The story centers on the main character, Susan Fletcher, a brilliant cryptographer working at the NSA. When she stumbles across a mysterious code on the NSA supercomputer TRANSLTR, Susan finds herself in a race against time to crack it and prevent catastrophe. As the plot progresses, betrayals are unmasked, secrets are revealed, and lives are put in danger.

The author, Dan Brown, uses his signature style of writing that combines fast action, technical details, and elements of suspense to keep readers immersed in the story. As the characters struggle to solve the riddle of the code and protect Digital Fortress, they are faced with ethical dilemmas and technological challenges that keep them on edge.

Although "Digital Fortress" is a work of fiction, the author strives to provide a basis of reality in his narrative by incorporating technical details and cryptography concepts. Although some of the descriptions and settings may be exaggerated or simplified to drive the plot forward, the book offers an intriguing perspective on the intersection of technology, security, and power.

It is important to note that, as a work of fiction, "Digital Fortress" seeks to entertain and captivate the reader rather than provide an accurate representation of technological and security reality. However, the novel serves as a starting point to explore relevant issues in the field of computer security and cryptography.

"Digital Fortress" is an exciting and immersive work that combines elements of technology, intrigue and suspense. Although it is a work of fiction, the author incorporates technical details and cryptography concepts to provide a fascinating experience. When reading the book, it is important to enjoy it as an entertaining story, but also to keep in mind that some aspects may be simplified or dramatized to serve the narrative purpose.

Dan Brown as Author

Dan Brown is a renowned mystery and thriller author, known for his ability to weave historical, artistic, and technological elements into his plots. His books are characterized by an agile and captivating narrative that keeps readers on edge until the last page.

In the case of "Digital Fortress," Brown demonstrates his skill in tackling topics related to technology and computer security, creating an exciting plot lined with intrigue. Although his novels fall within the fictional genre, Brown strives to provide a factual basis for his stories, meticulously researching and documenting to provide technical and scientific details that support his plot.

However, it's important to note that Brown is not an expert in technology or computer security, and his primary focus lies on entertainment and creating exciting suspense. This implies that some of the technical claims and descriptions in his works may be simplified or exaggerated to drive the plot forward and keep the reader's attention.

As an author, Dan Brown stands out for his ability to combine detailed research with fast-paced, immersive storytelling. His books have been widely popular, attracting a wide audience who appreciate his intriguing writing style full of unexpected twists and turns. In addition, his works have been adapted to the cinema, which demonstrates his impact and success in the literary world.

Dan Brown is a talented author who has managed to captivate readers with his stories full of suspense and mystery. Although his focus on technology and information security in "Digital Fortress" may not be entirely accurate from a technical perspective, his ability to weave fictional elements with real data and research creates an exciting and engaging writing experience.

Contributions of the book

"Digital Fortress" by Dan Brown is a novel that delves into the world of technology and computer security, presenting a plot full of intrigue and suspense. Although it is a work of fiction, the book offers some interesting contributions in these fields, although it is also far from reality in certain aspects.

One of the main contributions of the book is its ability to arouse the reader's interest and curiosity towards topics such as cryptography, security systems and data protection. Through compelling narrative, Brown makes readers think about the importance of computer security in our modern society.

The author introduces basic concepts about cryptography and encryption algorithms, presenting some principles and techniques used in the field of information security. While the information provided may be oversimplified or exaggerated to fit the plot, it serves as a starting point to get readers interested in further research on the topic.

In addition, "Digital Fortress" addresses ethical and moral issues related to privacy and access to personal information. Through the dilemmas faced by the characters, the book invites us to reflect on the limits of surveillance and the balance between security and individual freedom.

However, it is important to note that the book is a work of fiction and should not be taken as a manual or guide on computer security. Some of the depictions and technical descriptions may be simplified or exaggerated to create an atmosphere of tension and mystery in the plot.

Dan Brown's "Digital Fortress" offers a mix of fictional elements and concepts related to technology and computer security. Although it is not an accurate representation of reality, it manages to arouse the reader's interest in these issues and stimulates reflection on the importance of security in the digital world. It is important to approach the work with a critical mind and complement it with reliable and up-to-date sources to obtain a more complete understanding of the topics covered.

Plot elements with bias towards reality

The concept of reality-biased plot element refers to those elements or situations present in a literary work that are inspired by real life or approach verisimilitude. These elements, based on recognizable experiences, can generate empathy and a sense of identification in the reader (Cuddon, 2013).

Reality-biased plot elements add depth and credibility to the story, providing a sense of authenticity and allowing the reader to become more actively involved in the plot (Abrams & Harpham, 2014). These elements may include characters based on real people, historical events, or situations that reflect society and the world in which we live.

It is important to take into account that the trend towards reality can vary in different literary works and will depend on the author's approach and the literary genre to which the work belongs. Some authors opt for a more realistic representation of reality, while others use fantastic or surreal elements to convey their ideas (Booker, 2004).

In the novel "Digital Fortress" by Dan Brown, various situations are explored that are characterized by their tendency towards reality in the development of the plot. Throughout the work, elements are presented that are close to credibility and that allow the reader to immerse themselves in a world close to reality. In this review, we'll take a closer look at these elements and how they contribute to building a compelling and captivating narrative.

We'll explore how the author uses plausible, real-life situations to build an emotional connection with the characters and hold the reader's interest throughout the story. Furthermore, we will examine how these realistic elements intertwine with other more fictional aspects of the plot, creating a balance between the believable and the imaginary. Next, the different elements of the plot that present a tendency towards the real in the situations exposed by the novel "Digital Fortress" by Dan Brown are analyzed:

Kanji

Phrase from the book: Becker nodded. He explained that kanji was a Japanese writing system based on Chinese characters.

Description: Kanji, one of the three main components of the Japanese writing system, are ideograms inherited from Chinese characters. Each kanji has its own meaning and can represent a whole word on its own. Also, by combining kanjis, more complex words can be formed. For example, merging the kanji for "electricity" with that for "car" creates the word "train" (Seeley et al., 2009).

Unlike their use in Chinese, in Japanese, kanjis are used primarily to represent concepts. Each kanji acts as the semantic root of a word, while grammatical modifications, such as conjugations and derivations, are indicated by using the hiragana or katakana syllabaries, known as okurigana (Yasuoka, 2010).

The kanji writing system was adopted in Japan around the third century, and Japan has retained the traditional forms of these characters ever since, even after mainland China simplified them during the Cultural Revolution in the 1960s (Seeley et al., 2009).

It is estimated that there are more than 10,000 kanji characters, although it only takes between 2,000 and 3,000 to read a Japanese-language newspaper. In an effort to standardize and simplify the teaching and use of kanji, the Japanese government has officially designated a set of 1,945 characters as "everyday kanji" (Hadamitzky & Spahn, 2011).

Before the adoption of Chinese characters, there was no native writing system in Japan. When Chinese characters were adopted, Japanese incorporated both the original Chinese pronunciation (on yomi) and the corresponding Japanese pronunciation (kun yomi), adding an additional layer of complexity to the Japanese language (Yasuoka, 2010).

In modern Japanese, kanji are used to write nouns, adjectives, adverbs, and verbs. Unlike Chinese, however, Japanese cannot be written entirely in kanji. For grammatical purposes and for words that do not have a corresponding kanji, two additional syllabaries are used, known as hiragana and katakana, each consisting of 46 characters (Hadamitzky & Spahn, 2011).

Analysis: Dan Brown has done a remarkable job in his description of the kanji in the novel. By mentioning that kanji is a Japanese writing system based on Chinese characters, he is providing an accurate description.

Kanji is, in effect, one of the three writing systems used in the Japanese language, and it is true that it is based on Chinese characters. Kanji were introduced to Japan from China around the 5th century, and have since become deeply embedded in the linguistic and cultural fabric of Japanese.

Each kanji is an ideogram, that is, a symbol that represents a concept or idea. This concept can be a thing, a quality or a verb. Therefore, unlike an alphabet in which each character represents a sound and has no inherent meaning, each kanji is itself a carrier of meaning.

Therefore, the character Becker's claim in "Digital Fortress" that kanji is a Japanese writing system based on Chinese characters is completely accurate and provides a simplified but effective description of the kanji writing system.

1980s and email

Phrase from the book: During the 1980s and the advent of email.

Description: The eighties marked a milestone in the evolution of computer communications, mainly fostered by the dizzying technological advances of those years. It was in this period that they began to explore the foundations of a concept towards which we are inclined today: the integration of information (Leiner et al., 2009).

Thus, the notion of an Integrated Services Digital Network (ISDN) emerged, an infrastructure that aspired to consolidate all the forms of information that were transmitted in telecommunications at that time: voice, video, data, fax, in a single digital communication. This idea materialized in the early 1990s with the appearance of the first integrated digital networks in Europe, America and Japan, and today we have a well-established ISDN, although possibly already obsolete (ITU-T, 1988).

In the early to mid 1980s, we saw machines equipped with a modest number of vector processors working in parallel, which became the norm, with a typical number of processors ranging from 4 to 16. In the late 1980s and early In the 1990s, the focus shifted from vector processors to massively parallel processor systems with thousands of "common" CPUs (Dongarra & Sullivan, 2000). Currently, parallel designs are based on commonly available server microprocessors.

The concept of "public access" encompasses both access to technology (computer, connectivity, bandwidth, etc.) and access to all content stored on the world's largest artificial network, as the Internet has been characterized by Newsweek . Of these two aspects, the second precedes the first in importance, since technology is at the service of the content (knowledge) that it can transmit. It could be compared to supplying a village with water through a pipe: clearly, the water is more important than the pipes (Napoli, 2001).

Email, one of the earliest and most fundamental services on the Internet, arose from the ability to share information on a large scale, connecting everyone in the world. Currently, a person can have public access to the network and communicate with people in other parts of the world. When you send email, you are sending a message that is rarely intercepted, making it secure, fast, and reliable. Unfortunately, this also means that terrorists and other rogue groups can send large amounts of information undetected. During the 1980s, they realized the potential of electronic mail, and with the use of networks already in the public domain, this service became easier to use for the dissemination of messages through the network (Hauben & Hauben, 1997).

Analysis: The claim in Dan Brown's "Digital Fortress" that points to the arrival of email during the 1980s is partially true, but can be a bit misleading without additional context. Email, as a concept, actually dates back to before the 1980s.

The earliest forms of email can be traced back to the 1960s. In 1965, users of a time-share mainframe at MIT could leave messages for others who had access to the same machine, in what was perhaps one of the first email implementations. However, the system was limited as it only worked on a single machine.

In 1971, Ray Tomlinson, an engineer for the ARPANET (the forerunner of the Internet), created the first email system that allowed messages to be sent between machines. Tomlinson is also credited with introducing the "@" symbol to separate the user's name and the location of the mail server, a convention still in use today.

While these early implementations of email existed before the 1980s, it was during this period that email began to spread beyond universities and research labs. During the 1980s, businesses began to adopt email systems for internal use, and Internet service providers began offering email access as part of their services.

So while email certainly became more prominent and widely used during the 1980s, to say that it arrived during this period may not fully acknowledge the groundbreaking work that occurred in the preceding decades. In terms of "Digital Fortress", the importance of email in the plot, especially in terms of security and cryptography, reflects its increasing importance in society during this period.

Cryptography

Phrase from the book: encryption

Description: Cryptography is a fascinating field of study in computer science that amalgamates science, art, and technology. Although the word "encryption" may sound strange in Spanish, it is a frequently used term in the technical literature (Stallings, 2017).

Cryptography consists of two crucial elements: a message and a private access key that is shared between the sender and the receiver, which allows the decryption of the message. The cryptography process converts a message or file into an encrypted text (Menezes, 1997).

Cryptography is the process by which readable information is converted to an unreadable format to protect it. The information, once encrypted, can only be read by applying a key (Stallings, 2017).

It is a security measure used to store or transfer sensitive information that should not be accessible to third parties, such as passwords, credit card numbers, and private conversations, among others (Stallings, 2017).

The encryption process uses complex mathematical calculations, and to decrypt the information, a key must be used as a parameter to these formulas. The clear text that is encrypted is known as a cryptogram (Menezes, 1997).

For clarification, the use of the word "encryption" is preferred instead of "encryption", since the latter is a mistranslation of the English term "encrypt" (Stallings, 2017).

Analysis: In "Digital Fortress," Dan Brown tackles the concept of encryption with remarkably accurate fashion for a work of fiction. Encryption, as described in the book, is a process that converts readable information into an unreadable format to protect it. This is achieved using mathematical algorithms and a key that is needed to decrypt the information (Stallings, 2017). This description is consistent with the reality of how encryption works.

However, in the book's narrative, encryption is taken to a dramatic level with the creation of a tamper-proof encryption algorithm. In the real world, there is no such thing as a completely unbreakable algorithm. All encryption systems can be broken with enough time and computational resources. The security they provide is based on the fact that it would take years, decades or even centuries to crack the encryption with current technology, which makes it practically unfeasible (Menezes, Van Oorschot, & Vanstone, 1997).

Also, encryption in the real world is not a panacea for all security problems. Although you can protect the confidentiality of information, there are other security considerations that must be addressed, such as user authentication and data integrity.

In conclusion, while "Digital Fortress" provides a simplified and somewhat dramatized representation of encryption, its overview of how encryption works is pretty accurate. The book offers an accessible introduction to this complex topic, although readers should keep in mind that the reality of encryption and computer security is considerably more complicated.

three million processors

Phrase from the book: Its three million processors would work in parallel at blinding speed, trying one permutation after another.

Description: "Transltr" is a proposed supercomputer concept in Dan Brown's "Digital Fortress", which relies on the existence of actual supercomputers used by the NSA. Today, we have machines that can perform hundreds of trillion calculations per second, such as the NSA's "Black Widow" supercomputer. This is demonstrated by the current rankings of supercomputers, where each machine works in parallel with multiple processors. Therefore, it is not unreasonable to think that there are even faster computers than the fictional "Transltr" (Norton, 2022).

The "Transltr" in the book, a parallel-processing supercomputer with three million Freon-cooled processors, is an astonishing conception. To understand the scope of this idea, we can compare it with the world's most powerful supercomputer in reality, Fujitsu's "Fugaku", which has approximately 7.6 million CPU cores (Dongarra et al., 2021). Despite the literary hype, it is interesting to consider the possibility of a supercomputer of this magnitude.

Analysis: The idea that a supercomputer can have millions of processors working in parallel is actually quite accurate, although it may be a bit of a stretch in the case of the "Transltr" supercomputer described in "Digital Fortress".

In reality, the world's most powerful supercomputers use parallel processing to perform calculations at astonishing speed. Parallel processing allows multiple computations to be performed simultaneously, which increases the speed and efficiency of the computer. This is especially useful for tasks that require great computing power, such as simulating physical phenomena, processing large data sets, or, in the case of the NSA, decrypting encrypted information.

Fujitsu's "Fugaku", currently recognized as the world's most powerful supercomputer, has approximately 7.6 million CPU cores. Although this falls short of the "three million processors" described in the novel, it is still an impressive amount of processing power (Dongarra et al., 2021).

Thus, Dan Brown's claim in "Digital Fortress" that a supercomputer can have millions of processors working in parallel is technically feasible, although the exact number of three million may be a literary exaggeration.

Transltr capacity

Phrase from the book: TRANSLTR cracked hundreds of codes daily.

Description: According to Dan Brown's description in "Digital Fortress", the TRANSLTR supercomputer can test up to 30 million keys per second. If we take into account the 3 million processors that make it up, this would imply that each processor would try approximately 10 keys per second. Although this may not sound like impressive speed, it is important to consider the magnitude of the problem these processors face when attempting to crack encrypted keys (Brown, 1998).

However, some calculations in the book may not be accurate. For example, a 64-bit key has 2^{64} possible combinations, which is roughly 1.8×10^{19} distinct values. At a rate of 30 million keys per second, exploring all these combinations would take more than a million years (Diffie & Hellman, 1976). This suggests that TRANSLTR's performance, as described in the novel, might be overstated.

On the other hand, the real life supercomputer, IBM's Roadrunner, which was in operation between 2008 and 2013, was capable of speeds of 1 petaFLOP, that is, 10^{15} floating point operations per second (Feng et al., 2009). While this doesn't directly translate to the ability to test encryption keys, it does demonstrate that real-life supercomputers can achieve extremely high processing speeds.

Although some aspects of the TRANSLTR supercomputer and

its key-cracking capabilities may be literary exaggerations, real-life supercomputers have been shown to be capable of very high processing speeds.

Analysis: In the book "Digital Fortress" by Dan Brown, it is relevant to consider that the statement that "Transltr cracked hundreds of codes daily" is plausible, although highly dependent on the level of complexity of the codes to be cracked.

A quantum computer, like the one described in the work, would have a processing capacity vastly superior to that of conventional computers. In fact, it has been theoretically shown that quantum computers can break public-key cryptography used in the digital world today (Bernstein & Lange, 2017). Therefore, in theory, a machine as powerful as TRANSLTR might be able to crack hundreds of codes every day, assuming that these codes are not extraordinarily complex or long.

However, it is important to note that, in reality, practical and functional quantum computers are still in development, and their ability to break codes is still a matter of research and experimentation.

Although the claim that TRANSLTR can crack hundreds of codes daily may be theoretically plausible, current technology has not yet reached the level of performance described in the novel.

A mathematical impossibility

Phrase from the book: An indecipherable code is a mathematical impossibility! He knows!

Description: In one particular instance of "Digital Fortress", Susan Fletcher's character forcefully proclaims: "An indecipherable code is a mathematical impossibility." However, with all due respect, Dr. Fletcher's position is not entirely accurate. There is a cryptographic system known as the "One-Time Pad" (OTP) that is, in fact, unbreakable when used correctly. This encryption method is based on the "add" of a sequence of random characters to a clear text. We could visualize this as a simple equation of the type X+Y=Z, where X is the cleartext, Y is the one-time random key, and

Z is the resulting ciphertext (Singh, 1999).

For an adversary trying to decipher the message, the equation would reverse to X=ZY. For each "key" value Y, they would get a plaintext value X. But which one is correct? That is uncertain. In theory, any cleartext of the same length as the ciphertext is a possible solution, making it impossible to determine the true message without knowing the one-time key (Shannon, 1949). Thus, while it is true that many codes can be cracked with enough time and computing power, some cryptographic systems, such as the one-time passbook, can be effectively uncrackable if implemented correctly.

Analysis: In "Digital Fortress", one of the most striking statements is that "An indecipherable code is a mathematical impossibility!". However, the reality of cryptography and the mathematics behind it is somewhat more complicated.

It is true that, in practice, most encryption codes or systems can be broken with enough time, resources, and computational effort. Therefore, one could interpret the statement that there are no "unbreakable" codes as a reference to this reality. In fact, many encryption systems are designed to be "secure", which in this context usually means that cracking them without the correct key would require such a large computational effort that it would be practically unfeasible.

However, there is one important exception to this rule: the One-Time Pad, or One-Time Pad (OTP). An OTP is an encryption system that, if used correctly, is theoretically unbreakable. It works by combining the original message (the "clear text") with a secret key that is as long as the message itself and is used only once. If the key is truly random, and if it is kept secret and never used again, then the OTP is uncrackable, even in principle.

Thus, the claim that "An indecipherable code is a mathematical impossibility!" It is not completely correct, since there are encryption systems, such as OTP, which are theoretically indecipherable. However, the statement does capture an important reality of modern cryptography, which is that most ciphers can be cracked given enough resources and time.

brute force attack

Phrase from the book: a brute force attack. PGP, Lucifer, DSA, it doesn't matter.

Description: Brute force attack, a tactic commonly used in cryptography, involves trying all possible key combinations until the correct one is found. This is done by applying the encryption algorithm to one of the elements of a cleartext/encrypted pair, using every possible key combination, until the other member of the pair is obtained. Theoretically, the effort required for the search to succeed with a probability better than chance will require $2^n - 1$ operations, where n is the length of the key, a concept also known as the space of keys (Katz & Lindell, 2014).

However, in "Digital Fortress", Dan Brown depicts the TRANSLTR supercomputer as a machine capable of breaking through any encryption barrier, regardless of the algorithm used. This representation, although exciting for the plot of the novel, deviates from technological and mathematical reality. In practice, the decryption of a key generally requires prior knowledge of the algorithm used for its encryption, and it is unlikely that a key will be decrypted without this information (Schneier, 1996).

Also, algorithms like PGP, DES (formerly known as Lucifer), and DSA are different from each other and use different encryption methods. For example, PGP uses the RSA algorithm, which is asymmetric, while DES, proposed by the NSA, is a symmetric algorithm. DSA, on the other hand, is not an encryption standard but rather a standard for digital signatures (Diffie & Landau, 2007). Each of these algorithms has a specific method of encryption and decryption, which means that you need to know the algorithm used to encrypt the key in order to decrypt it.

Analysis: The phrase "a brute force attack. PGP, Lucifer, DSA, it doesn't matter" points to the idea that any encryption, no matter how complex or the specific algorithm it uses, can be defeated by a brute force attack.

In cryptographic terms, a brute force attack refers to the tactic of trying all possible key combinations until the correct one is discovered. This is a time-consuming method, and depending on the length of the key and the computational power of the attacker, it can be an extremely long and resource-intensive process (Katz & Lindell, 2014).

The aforementioned algorithms—PGP, Lucifer (now known as DES), and DSA—are all encryption or authentication methods with different features and levels of security. For example, PGP and Lucifer/DES are both encryption algorithms, but they use different approaches (asymmetric and symmetric, respectively) to encrypt and decrypt messages. DSA, on the other hand, is an algorithm used for message authentication, not encryption (Schneier, 1996).

In theory, it is true that any encryption could be broken by a brute force attack. However, this assumes that the attacker has unlimited computing resources and unlimited time. In practice, many modern ciphers are robust enough to withstand a brute force attack within a reasonable amount of time. For example, a strong encryption with a 128-bit key would have 2^{128} possible key combinations, a number so large that it would take many years, even with the most powerful supercomputers, to try all the combinations (Diffie & Landau, 2007). .

Therefore, while it is true that a brute force attack can, in theory, defeat any encryption, in practice this is not always the case. Additionally, it is important to note that the choice of encryption algorithm can have a significant impact on data security.

self-encryption

Phrase from the book: Is Digital Fortress self-encrypted?

Description: A self-encryption is a type of encryption that embeds the original message (the plaintext) in the encryption key. There are two main ways to implement self-encryption: using a key autoclave and text self-encryption. In a self-encrypting key, the previous components of the key stream determine the next element in the key stream. On the other hand, a text self-encryption uses the previous message to decide the next element of the keystream. In contemporary cryptography, auto-synchronization stream ciphers are essentially self-encrypting (Stinson, 2006).

Modern self-encryptors use various encryption methods, but they all take advantage of the same principle of using existing key bytes or plaintext bytes to generate more key bytes. Newer stream ciphers are based on pseudorandom number generators, in which the key is used to initialize the generator, and both key and text bytes are fed back into the generator to produce more bytes (Menezes et al. ., 1997).

Some stream ciphers are called "self-encrypting" since the next byte of the key generally depends only on the previous N bytes of the message. If a byte in the message is lost or corrupted, the keystream will also be corrupted, but only until all N bytes have been processed. From that moment on, the key flow returns to normal and the rest of the message is decrypted correctly (Schneier, 1996).

Generally, a code or message is not automatically encrypted, although it is possible for a program or virus to encrypt itself to avoid detection by other programs that analyze the character sequences they generate. As mentioned above, this process is known as generating autoclaves or autoclaved texts from the initial key. In this sense, Digital Fortress can be considered as a type of program, similar to a keylogger, that generates random keys and updates itself every time it generates a key, so the term used in the book is appropriate (Brown, 1998).

Analysis: In Dan Brown's book "Digital Fortress", the idea that a program or system is "self-encrypting" is a literary interpretation of various cryptography and computer security concepts. In the real world, self-encryption is not a commonly used practice in computer security, but it is a concept that can be explored and understood.

In cryptographic terms, self-encryption refers to the idea that a program or system can encrypt its own data or code, often with the goal of protecting against unauthorized access or analysis by third parties. This is technically possible and is used in certain contexts, such as malware that encrypts itself to avoid detection by antivirus software. However, self-encryption is a complex process and is not a guarantee of absolute security.

In "Digital Fortress", "self-encryption" is used more as a plot device to create tension and mystery. It's important to remember that while Brown does a good job of incorporating cryptography and computer security concepts into his novel, it's still a work of fiction and not everything strictly adheres to reality.

So while the idea that "Digital Fortress" is "self-encrypting" may be exciting in the context of the novel, it is not necessarily reflected in the actual practice of cryptography and computer security. In a real sense, self-encryption is more of a theoretical concept than a commonly used practice.

Send emails to a dead account

Phrase from the book: Tankado may have been sending fake emails to a dead account.

Description: If you thought your inbox was shielded against threats, think again. A new breed of spam lurks in the shadows, a breed that is not only annoying and annoying, but also an open door for the theft of sensitive data such as credit card numbers, passwords, account details, and other personal information. Read on to better understand this new modality of theft and how to safeguard your personal data (Acquisti et al., 2004).

Have you heard of "phishing"? It is a fraud method that aims to steal your identity. This crime involves the acquisition of information such as credit card numbers, passwords, account details and other personal data through deception. This form of fraud often reaches people through unsolicited emails or pop-ups (Dingledine et al., 2004).

Phishing can even target what are known as "dead" email accounts. But what exactly does that mean? In simple terms, a "dead" email account is one that no longer exists or has been deleted. However, since a "dead" account is no longer active, any messages sent to it will be rejected. This usually results in a bounce email from the mail server, often from an address like " postmasterdelivery@mail.com ", notifying that the message could not be delivered. In short, it is not possible to send emails to "dead" accounts (Levine et al., 2009).

Analysis: When analyzing the sentence "Tankado may have been sending fake emails to a dead account" from Dan Brown's book

"Digital Fortress", it is important to consider some technological and contextual aspects to assess its plausibility.

In computer terms, a "dead account" refers to an email address that is no longer active, that is, it has been deactivated or deleted. In practice, if you try to send an email to a dead account, the mail server usually rejects the delivery and returns an error message to the sender, indicating that the email address does not exist or is not available.

So why would Tankado, a character with advanced computer skills, send mail to a dead account? There are several possibilities that could be adjusted to reality.

One possibility is that Tankado was using the dead account as some kind of decoy or diversion. By sending emails to an inactive account, he may have been trying to mislead those who might be tracking his online activity. In fact, it's a well-known tactic in the cybersecurity world: while it may seem useless to send emails to a dead account, it can actually serve as a form of digital "noise" to hide other, more significant actions.

Another possibility is that Tankado was testing some kind of exploit or hacking technique. In some cases, hackers can find ways to "revive" dead accounts or access information that may still be associated with them, even after they've been deactivated.

So while it may seem unlikely or useless at first glance to send emails to a dead account, there are circumstances in which this action could have a strategic purpose. In this sense, Brown's claim in "Digital Fortress" is not entirely unrelated to reality, especially in the context of a high-tech thriller and computer espionage. However, as always, the exact reality of these tactics would depend on the specific circumstances and technologies at play.

Spain is not the capital of cryptography

Phrase from the book: Why not? Spain is by no means the world capital of cryptography. No one would know what the letters meant. Furthermore, if the password is the usual sixty-four bits, even in daylight no one would be able to read and memorize all sixty-four characters.

Description: Questioning the choice of Spain as a scenario for cryptography can arise for several reasons, but it is important to remember that cryptography is not limited to a particular region; it is not anchored to a single global epicenter (Katz, Lindell, 2014). In fact, even if Spain is not widely recognized as a crypto beacon, any location is perfectly viable considering the basic principles of cryptography.

On the other hand, the mention of a 64-bit access key is relevant. In terms of computer security, a 64-bit password is long and complex, and even if displayed in broad daylight, it would be virtually impossible for a casual observer to read and memorize all 64 characters without help (Stallings, 2017). It is a testament to the effectiveness of key length in protecting encrypted information.

Analysis: The quote presented in Dan Brown's "Digital Fortress" raises several interesting questions from a realistic analysis perspective.

"Spain is not even close to the world capital of cryptography": This is true. Although Spain has contributed in various fields of technology and science, it is not particularly recognized as a global epicenter of cryptography. However, this does not limit the possibility of significant crypto events taking place in Spain, as cryptography is a global discipline and is not limited to a specific geographic location.

"No one would know what the letters meant": This may be true to a large extent. Cryptography, by its nature, is a specialized field and not everyone is familiar with its terminology and techniques. Unless someone has training or an interest in the field, they probably won't understand encrypted characters or codes.

"If the password has the usual sixty-four bits, even in daylight no one would be able to read and memorize all sixty-four characters": This is pretty accurate. A 64-bit key, which would translate to 64 alphanumeric characters, would be very difficult for most people to memorize. Also, without the correct knowledge or context of the key, even if someone could read it, it would have no meaning to them.

In general, this sentence seems quite realistic in terms of the representation of cryptography and its complexity. However, it is important to remember that while cryptography can be a complex and specialized field, awareness and understanding of it is growing as digital technology becomes more central to our lives.

automobile with gagets

Phrase from the book: Greg Hale, his car was a showpiece: he had installed a global positioning system, voice-activated door locks, a radar jammer, and a fax and telephone system to always be in contact with his answering machines. His vain license plate read MEGABITS, and was framed in neon purple.

Description: Greg Hale, a fictional character in Dan Brown's "Digital Fortress," is named after several real-life figures, including a Greg Hale who seems to excel in the field of cryptography. This individual, a PhD from York University, has made significant contributions to the field of Human-Computer Interaction and Computer Assisted Learning (Hale, G., 2023).

In the novel, Hale owns a vehicle equipped with voice recognition, a technology that not only exists today, but has advanced significantly. Originally implemented by IBM, this system allows you to control various vehicle functions through voice commands, such as asking for the nearest service station or requesting the fastest route (IBM, 2020).

Hale also has a car alarm activated by GPS, a system that allows you to control the vehicle's lock through a cell phone. In addition, the use of radar jamming systems, which can jam radio signals, is mentioned, and although their use is illegal due to their interference with other devices, it is hinted that Hale may have used them for evasion purposes (Smith, J. , 2021).

A landline telephone can be installed in Hale's vehicle, which implies the possibility of connecting faxes in the car. Although mobile phones are more common today, mobile technologies such as mobile faxes and mobile printers are a reality. For example, Greta GMS is a mobile device that acts as a printer, fax, and GSM phone (Greta, 2022).

Analysis: The elements described in this sentence are, to a great extent, possible and resemble the current reality, although with certain nuances.

First of all, the Global Positioning System (GPS) is a technology that has become ubiquitous in modern vehicles. GPS systems allow drivers to accurately navigate to their destinations and can also be used to track a vehicle's location in real time.

Voice-activated door locks also exist, although they are not common on most vehicles today. However, with the rise of artificial intelligence and the integration of voice assistants like Alexa, Siri and Google Assistant into cars, this technology is becoming more and more feasible.

Radar jammers, although they exist, are illegal in many countries due to their potential to interfere with signals from police radars and other important security systems. Although Greg Hale might have the ability to install such a device, using it in real life would carry serious legal repercussions.

As for an in-vehicle phone and fax system, this was more common in the 1980s and 1990s, before the popularization of mobile phones. Today, with the rise of digital communication, a fax system in a vehicle would be considered obsolete. However, the ability to be in constant communication is very feasible with today's technology, from calls to video conferences, everything is possible through smartphones and mobile networks.

Personalized "MEGABITS" license plate and neon purple frame are entirely possible, although the legality and availability of personalized plates varies by country. Overall, the description of Greg Hale's car is a good example of how today's technology can be used (or misused) in a modern car, although some items, like the radar jammer, would be illegal or impractical in the modern car. real life.

Single public key encryption standard

Phrase from the book: Four years earlier, in an effort to create a single standard for public key encryption, Congress commissioned the best mathematicians in the country, those at the NSA, to develop a new algorithm. The plan was for Congress to pass legislation that would make that new algorithm the norm for the nation, thus alleviating the incompatibilities suffered by companies using different algorithms. The NSA's cryptography team, led by Commander Strathmore, reluctantly created an algorithm they named Skipjack and presented it to Congress for approval.

Description: In the context of cryptography and information security, it is essential to talk about the Clipper Chip and its associated algorithm, Skipjack, key elements in the history of communications security (Abelson et al., 1997). The Clipper Chip, a microprocessor developed by the US National Security Agency (NSA) in 1993, was designed to be used in telecommunications devices for encrypted voice transmission (Schneier, 1994).

The Skipjack algorithm, also developed by the NSA, was initially of a classified nature, so it was not subject to conventional reviews by the world cryptographic community. It was known to use an 80-bit encryption key, which was a symmetric algorithm, similar to the DES encryption algorithm. It was declassified and published in 1998 (Bellovin & Blaze, 1996). According to sources at the time, the initial cost of the microprocessor ranged from $16 (unprogrammed) to $26 (programmed), and the chip was manufactured by Mykotronx and VLSI Technology, Inc.

The fundamental concept of the Clipper Chip and Skipjack was the "Key Escrow" or locked key. This concept implied that any device using the Clipper Chip would receive a "cryptographic key" that would be given to the government as "guarantee" (Diffie & Landau, 2007). If a government agency deemed it necessary to listen to an encrypted communication, the key would be unlocked and given to decrypt the communication.

Despite the government's attempts to regulate the use of encryption algorithms, resistance and criticism arose from civil organizations and companies. Organizations such as the Electronic Privacy Information Center and the Electronic Frontier Foundation challenged the Clipper Chip proposal, arguing that the move would leave citizens exposed to illegal government surveillance and possible security flaws in the algorithm, which could not be independently reviewed (EFF, 1994).

Senator John Ashcroft was a leading government opponent of the Clipper Chip, defending the right of individuals to encrypt their communications and the export of encryption software. In response to the government's proposal, software programs such as Nautilus, PGP, and PGPfone were developed, offering powerful and free encryption solutions. The crypto community believed that if these alternatives became widespread, the government would not be able to prevent their use. Eventually, the concept of "Key Escrow" in its Clipper Chip format fell out of favor (Schneier, 1996).

Analysis: Dan Brown's "Digital Fortress" quote has some foundation in historical events, but it has been embellished and simplified for the novel's plot.

In real life, the US National Security Agency (NSA) did develop an encryption algorithm called Skipjack in the 1990s, but it did not go at the behest of Congress to create a "single public key encryption standard." . Rather, it was part of a government security initiative called the Clipper Chip (Abelson et al., 1997). This chip was designed to be used in telecommunications devices and used the Skipjack algorithm for encryption.

An important detail is that Skipjack is a symmetric encryption algorithm, not a public key. The distinction is crucial in cryptography: public key algorithms use a key pair for encryption and decryption, while symmetric algorithms use the same key for both processes (Schneier, 1996).

Additionally, legislation intended to make Skipjack the national standard did not come to fruition. The effort was met with strong opposition from both the crypto community and the technology industry, largely due to privacy and security concerns (Diffie & Landau, 2007).

So while the book captures some truths about the development of Skipjack and the US government's efforts to control encryption, it does oversimplify and embellish the events quite a bit for plot purposes. It is important to remember that "Digital Fortress" is a work of fiction and, although it uses elements of reality to construct its plot, it should not be seen as an exact representation of historical events.

Telephone number length

Phrase from the book: Thirty-four sixty-two ten,' said the voice.

Description: Telephone numbering patterns vary globally and, although the most commonly recognized international standard for telephone numbers is generally seven digits, there are notable exceptions in different regions of the world, including Madrid and other cities, where it is possible to find numbers six-digit phone numbers (Ofcom, 2012).

Take, for example, the number +34 917 710 519. Breaking it down, we see that "34" is the country code, in this case, Spain, and "91" is the area code for Madrid. The "7" below may denote a more specific geographic subdivision, perhaps a neighborhood or region within Madrid. The remaining number, "10519", made up of five digits, would be the specific telephone line number. In this case, if we strictly refer to the line number, we would be talking about a five-digit number, not six.

Now, when in Spain, it is possible to dial just the line number (for example, 710 519) or the line number together with the area code (for example, 91 710 519). In the latter case, we would effectively be dialing a seven-digit number.

However, it is possible that in the original conversation, the speaker was referring only to the line number, omitting the country and area codes that are constant and predictable, and focusing on the digits that change from line to line. It is common practice to talk about telephone numbers in terms of their variable component, the line number (ITU-T, 2011).

Analysis: In "Digital Fortress", Dan Brown offers a fascinating insight into information technology and its role in cryptography and information security. As part of this approach, elements may be presented that, while based on fact and technological realities, may be adapted or exaggerated for the novel's plot.

As for the length of the phone numbers mentioned in the book, the reality is that it varies enormously around the world. The international telephone numbering system, established by the International Telecommunication Union, assigns each country a country code, and then each country has its own internal numbering system.

For example, in the United States and Canada, telephone numbers generally have ten digits: three for the area code, three for the area code, and four for the line number. However, in other countries, the numbers may be shorter or longer. Some countries even use variable length numbers.

In the case of Spain, which is specifically mentioned in "Digital Fortress", the standard is nine digits for telephone numbers, not counting the country code. This includes the area code and the line number. However, when speaking locally, area codes are often omitted and only line numbers are used, which can be 6 or 7 digits, depending on the specific location and type of line (landline or mobile).

So, the mention of phone number lengths in "Digital Fortress" fits the bill, but also requires a bit of context to fully understand. Telephone numbering systems are complex and vary from place to place, which can lead to some confusion if statements about the length of telephone numbers are taken literally.

LIMBO language was based on C and Pascal

Phrase from the book: Hale understood the LIMBO programming language well enough to know that it was based on two others, C and Pascal, that he did know.

Description: Emerging as a central theme in Dan Brown's "Digital Fortress" is the use of the LIMBO programming language, originally designed for the INFERNO operating system (Pike et al., 1995). It is interesting to note that, as suggested in the work, this language adopts significant elements from two other programming languages: C and Pascal.

The LIMBO language bears clear similarities to these two languages, a fact that resonates throughout the novel. In fact, there is evidence that some of the language constructions are similar to those of Pascal and his successors (Wirth, 1973). However, programmers are more likely to find a greater familiarity with C, since most LIMBO structures are based on this language, albeit in a more simplified form (Kernighan & Ritchie, 1978).

Therefore, it seems safe to conclude that LIMBO, as presented in "Digital Fortress", does indeed have roots in these two programming languages. The simplification it presents suggests a pragmatic approach to making the language more manageable and accessible.

Analysis: In "Digital Fortress", Dan Brown's claim that the LIMBO programming language is based on C and Pascal presents an interesting interpretation of the origins of this computer language. There is arguably some truth to this statement, but also some simplifications that might require further analysis. The LIMBO language was developed for the INFERNO operating system, as a concurrent programming language and designed for distributed systems. It is true that it has certain similarities to C and Pascal, in terms of syntax and structure. In LIMBO, one can find elements of procedure and structure that are reminiscent of Pascal (Wirth, 1973), and many aspects of control flow and variable declaration that seem to be influenced by C (Kernighan & Ritchie, 1978).

However, this is a somewhat simplified picture. While C and Pascal certainly left their mark on LIMBO, the latter also incorporates unique features that set it apart from its predecessors, such as its focus on concurrent programming and interprocess communication. Furthermore, LIMBO introduces a simplified and more manageable form of programming that can be considered an evolution of the ideas presented in C and Pascal, rather than simply an amalgamation of the two. Although Brown's statement has merit and offers a general idea of LIMBO's heritage, one should be aware that this language also offers unique features and advances that set it apart from its putative progenitors. Still, this description serves as an effective introduction for lay readers, providing programming context that may be easier to understand.

Sys-Sec

Phrase from the book: Sys-Sec, of course, did not have permission to access the information in the data bank, but was responsible for its security. Like all vast data banks, from insurance companies to universities, the NSA was continually attacked by hackers trying to get a peek into the secrets it held. But the NSA's computer firewall programmers were the best in the world. No one had succeeded in infiltrating the agency's data bank, and the NSA had no reason to suspect that anyone might.

As the Security agency is one of the largest in the world, or perhaps the largest, it is obvious that it is attacked by hackers from all over the world, trying to collect important and hidden information from the NSA, Sys-Sec is a security company for all types of systems, and wireless and wired networks, the only company that deals with security corresponding to this name is this company, from the ETH group in Zurich. It is not an integrated part of the NSA as mentioned in the book, but it is in charge of all kinds of security.

Description: The security of the National Security Agency (NSA) is a crucial topic that is explored in detail in "Digital Fortress" by Dan Brown. A particularly significant incident occurred on December 15, 2009, when a large-scale computer attack against the NSA was carried out, attributed to hackers from China (Zetter, 2014). This attack, carried out by sending malicious emails, demonstrated that even the NSA, despite its extensive security measures, is not invulnerable.

China allegedly carried out these attacks as a show of cybersecurity power, thereby exposing vulnerabilities within the NSA's security stronghold. This serves to illustrate that despite the NSA's robust cybersecurity infrastructure, there are persistent and increasingly sophisticated threats.

It is important to note that the NSA serves as a crucial cybersecurity shield for America, functioning as a firewall that filters and monitors a large amount of information entering and leaving the country (Bamford, 2012). Its responsibilities are vast, extending to all signals, home and public networks, and even utility systems such as gas, electricity, and sewage. However, as the 2009 attack demonstrates, no entity, no matter how powerful, is immune to the threat of cybersecurity.

Analysis: The term "Sys-Sec" appears to be an abbreviation for

"System Security", a commonly used phrase in the cybersecurity field. In practice, it refers to the measures and protocols established to protect computer systems and networks from possible threats. It is a vital element in any organization that depends on information technology, especially entities like the National Security Agency (NSA) mentioned in the book.

In the context of "Digital Fortress", the term is likely used to refer to a group or department within the NSA that deals with system security. This interpretation is consistent with the actual organization of many security agencies and private companies, where Systems Security (Sys-Sec) teams are an essential part of the cybersecurity infrastructure.

Brown's reference to "Sys-Sec" is quite accurate and reflects the importance of system security in the world of information technology. Although the specific organization and protocols of system security teams are likely to vary between different organizations, Brown's use of this term provides a realistic portrait of how these teams function in the real world.

TRANSLTR Power Consumption

Phrase from the book: TRANSLTR has been running at full power. Electricity consumption already exceeds half a million kilowatts per hour since midnight.

Description: Despite the fictional existence of the TRANSLTR supercomputer in Dan Brown's "Digital Fortress", it is undeniable that the National Security Agency (NSA) has a colossal power consumption. The NSA is reportedly the second largest consumer of electricity in the state of Maryland (Bamford, 2008).

The NSA headquarters, located in Fort Meade, Maryland, is only about 10 miles northwest of Washington DC as the crow flies. This strategic location is accessible through an exclusive exit on the Baltimore-Washington Expressway, reserved for NSA employees. The size of the NSA's operations is staggering, but can be inferred from its electricity consumption. With annual energy expenditure exceeding $21 million, it is clear that the scale of the NSA's operation is monumental (Bamford, 2012).

This figure translates into a monthly expenditure of approximately $1.75 million, suggesting an astronomical kilowatt-hour consumption, potentially exceeding even the figures mentioned in Brown's novel. Given the size of the organization and its energy consumption, this assumption is reasonable. The size of the NSA's infrastructure is evident in photographs showing around 18,000 parking spaces at its facilities.

Analysis: Analyzing the power consumption of the fictional TRANSLTR supercomputer, as described in Dan Brown's "Digital Fortress", is an intriguing undertaking. According to the book, TRANSLTR is a machine of incredible power and complexity, which would certainly be very energy intensive.

In real life, supercomputers are high-performance devices that consume large amounts of power. For example, the Summit supercomputer, which is located at the Oak Ridge National Laboratory in the United States and was one of the most powerful until my last update in September 2021, consumes approximately 13 megawatts of power (DoE, 2018). That's enough to power several thousand homes.

So it's not surprising that the fictional Transltr supercomputer, which according to the book has the ability to break any code in record time, has massive power consumption. While the book does not provide hard numbers, TRANSLTR's representation of power consumption largely aligns with the reality of today's supercomputers.

That being said, it is important to mention that modern supercomputers are also constantly being optimized to be more energy efficient, as power consumption is one of the main constraints in the development of these machines. Therefore, a fully accurate representation of TRANSLTR's power consumption would also have to consider these optimization efforts.

Calculated immediate of the probabilities

Phrase from the book: He calculated the probabilities in an instant: twenty-six raised to the fifth power: 11,881,376 possible choices. At one election per second, it would take nineteen weeks...

Description: The probability calculation made by Susan in the book "Digital Fortress" by Dan Brown is correct. She used the method of combining all the letters of the alphabet in each position of the key. Since there are 26 letters in the English alphabet and the key consists of 5 positions, the total number of possible keys would be 26 raised to the fifth power, which equals 11,881,376 possible combinations. Another option would be to consider that a character is represented by one byte, which in turn corresponds to 2^8 or 256 possibilities. If the key consists of 40 bits, there would be 2^{40} possible solutions.

These methods of calculating probabilities and chances in cryptography are valid and are used to assess the strength of encryption systems. Combining different letters or symbols in key positions and using bits to represent possible solutions are common approaches in cryptography and security analysis (Stallings, 2017).

It is important to consider that, in practice, cryptographic security is based on the difficulty of brute forcing all possible combinations to decrypt a message. The greater the number of possible keys, the more time and resources will be required to break the security of the system.

Analysis: In Dan Brown's book "Digital Fortress", it is mentioned that Susan quickly calculated the probabilities using the formula twenty-six to the fifth power, resulting in 11,881,376 possible choices. Based on the context, it is posited that if one choice were made per second, it would take her nineteen weeks to complete all possible combinations.

In general terms, the calculation of probabilities and the concept of possible combinations are in line with reality. The aforementioned calculation reflects a brute force technique in which all combinations of letters of the alphabet in each position of a key are considered.

It is important to note that the feasibility of this approach in practice depends on various factors, such as the processing power of the computer used, the specific encryption algorithm, and the security countermeasures implemented. In some cases, encryption systems may require much longer test times due to additional protection techniques such as hashing and salting.

Although the quoted figure for possible choices and the estimated time to complete them may vary based on multiple factors, the underlying idea of the calculation and analysis of probabilities is consistent with the principles of cryptography and security assessment.

Fictional plot elements

In literary narrative, the term fictionalized plot element refers to those components of a story that are not strictly based on reality, but are the product of the author's imagination. These elements can be characters, events, settings, technologies, among others, that do not exist in the real world, or that have been modified or exaggerated for the purpose of the plot.

This is due to the fact that fiction is not an imitation of real life, but an artistic construction that uses reality as a base. Paraphrasing Delany, we can say that fiction is not a mere representation of reality, but an artistic representation of reality. The author uses elements of reality and alters, exaggerates, or makes them up entirely to create a story that is interesting, exciting, or moving (Delany, 2006).

Fictional biased plot elements are essential in literature because they allow us to explore concepts, ideas, and possibilities that go beyond the constraints of the real world. They allow us to dream of what could be, explore different worlds and societies, and examine human behavior and social relationships in extreme or unusual situations.

Fictional biased plot elements are no less valuable than reality biased plot elements. Actually, they are just as important in creating a plot that is both entertaining and intellectually stimulating. The selected elements of the plot with this tendency are analyzed below:

Intelligence quotient

Phrase from the book: It is hard to imagine that they maintain an Intelligence Quotient of 170.

Description: Intellectual quotient, commonly known as CI (or IQ), is a score derived from a series of standardized tests intended to quantify intelligence (Gregory, 2004). Currently, various tests are used, such as the Wechsler Adult Intelligence Scale, which calculate the IQ based on the projection of the range of abilities of an individual in a normal distribution or Gaussian bell. With a mean value of 100 and a standard deviation of 15, those with IQs greater than 100 are considered above average, while those with IQs less than 100 are below average (Deary et al., 2001).

The term "gifted" is used to describe those who exceed 98% of the population in terms of IQ, which means that their scores fall at the far end of the normal distribution curve (Webb et al., 2007). A notable example of this is William James Sidis, who reportedly had an IQ of 300, although the validity of this claim is debated.

During the 1920s, the American psychologist Catherine M. Cox published a study in which she estimated the IQ of famous people from history between 1450 and 1850, based on biographical data (Cox, 1926). Some of the more notable estimates include Johann Wolfgang von Goethe (CI 210), Gottfried Leibniz (CI 205), Thomas Wolsey (CI 200), Blaise Pascal (CI 195), Sir Isaac Newton (CI 190), Galileo Galilei (CI 185), Leonardo da Vinci (CI 180) and René Descartes (CI 180), among others.

It is said that the person with the highest recorded IQ in the world is Marilyn vos Savant, an American writer whose IQ is 68 points higher than that of Albert Einstein (Colom, 2004). Vos Savant is recognized worldwide and has been classified as the most intelligent woman in the world, thanks to a registered coefficient of 128 points above the average, which has led her to be recognized in the Guinness Records.

The normal range for an IQ is between 80 and 110. An IQ is calculated by taking various tests to determine "mental age," which is then divided by chronological age and multiplied by 100 (Kaufman & Lichtenberger, 2006). Therefore, an IQ of 170 is extraordinarily high, 70 points above average. However, there are people like Marilyn who have even higher IQs.

Analysis: In "Digital Fortress", Dan Brown introduces characters with exceptional intellectual abilities, even going so far as to mention that some have an IQ of 170. To put this in perspective, it is estimated that around 99.997% of the population has an IQ below 170, which means that only a few people in every million would reach this number (Neisser et al., 1996).

It is important to understand that IQ is only a measure of cognitive ability and does not guarantee success in all areas of life.

While a high IQ may indicate an exceptional ability to learn, reason, and solve problems, it does not necessarily correlate with creativity, wisdom, judgment, or empathy.

Also, IQ is not an absolute measure of intelligence. IQ tests are designed to compare a person's cognitive ability with that of others in their age group, and results can be affected by a number of factors, including physical and mental health, education level, and age. cultural and socioeconomic environment (Neisser et al., 1996).

Therefore, while it is theoretically possible for a character in "Digital Fortress" to have an IQ of 170, this would be extremely rare. Furthermore, such a high IQ would not necessarily guarantee the kind of exceptional abilities that Dan Brown describes in his book. A character with an IQ of 170 would be extraordinarily intelligent, but intelligence alone does not guarantee the ability to solve the complex and multifaceted challenges presented in the novel's plot.

substitution cipher

Phrase from the book: XP UBNCJFO

Description: In the passage in the book in question, Dan Brown employs an encryption method known as substitution, a process of replacing characters from the original message with others according to a specific pattern, thus generating an encoded sequence that can be deciphered by someone who know the pattern (Singh, 1999).

In a communication between the characters Susan and David, Susan creates a message using a substitution cipher. In her method, each letter of the original message is replaced by the next letter in the alphabet. For example, a 'B' would become 'C', and so on. By following this pattern, David was able to unravel the coded message.

In his answer, David employs a similar technique, but with a twist. In his cipher, each letter is replaced by the one that precedes it in the alphabet: if an 'R' appears, it becomes 'Q'. However, this coding system presents an anomaly with the letter 'X', which instead of being replaced by 'Y' as one would expect, is changed to 'W'. This fact indicates a flaw in the encryption logic, a reminder that although this encryption method may seem simple, it is still subject to errors and inconsistencies.

Analysis: The phrase "XP UBNCJFO" from Dan Brown's "Digital Fortress" appears to be an example of a message encrypted with a substitution cipher, most likely a Caesar cipher.

The Caesar cipher is one of the oldest and simplest encryption methods, where each letter in the plaintext is 'shifted' a certain number of places in the alphabet (Singh, 1999). In this case, as mentioned in your description, David uses a shift back one letter in the alphabet to encrypt his message. Therefore, if we apply this encryption logic to the phrase "XP UBNCJFO", each letter would be moved one position forward in the alphabet to be decrypted. However, as you mention, there is an exception with the letter 'X', which instead of being replaced by 'Y', is changed to 'W'.

Thus, if we decrypt "XP UBNCJFO" following the general forward shift rule and considering the exception for 'X', we get "WO TOBMEIN". However, if we consider that 'X' should be shifted to 'W', we get "WO VOBMEIN". Both decryptions do not appear to be meaningful in English, suggesting that the message may be in another language, has been encrypted in another way, or is in error.

Since the description of the encryption method used in the book is clear, the phrase "XP UBNCJFO" should have been easily cracked. However, the interpretation of this sentence is not self-evident, suggesting that the representation of the substitution cipher in "Digital Fortress" may be in error, or that there may be some additional detail not mentioned that is crucial to correctly understanding the message.

transltr the supercomputer

Phrase from the book: TRANSLTR Dan Brown's supercomputer, reality or fantasy?

Description: The concept of a supercomputer, such as the one described in Dan Brown's "Digital Fortress," TRANSLTR (an acronym for "Translator Super Computer" or "Translation Super Computer"), is a product of fiction. There is no such device in reality, although it is true that computers exist that can process data at extraordinarily high speeds. Some of these state-of-the-art systems are described below:

The Franklin supercomputer, a 2.3 GHz Cray XT Quadcore installed in 2008 at NERSC/LBNL, Berkeley, California, has a processing capacity of 266 Teraflops and a memory of 77280 GB (TOP500, 2008).

Another impressive machine is the Ranger, a SunBlade x6420, Opteron QC 2.3 Ghz, Infiniband, located at the Texas Advanced Computing Center at the University of Texas. It was installed in 2008 and has a processing capacity of 433.2 Teraflops and a memory of 125952 GB (TOP500, 2008).

At Argonne National Laboratory, Illinois, is the Blue Gene/P Solution, installed in 2007, with a processing capacity of 450.3 Teraflops (Argonne National Laboratory, 2007).

In Livermore, California, there is the Blue Gene/L, installed in 2007, with a processing capacity of 478.2 Teraflops and a memory of 73728 GB (DOE/NNSA/LLNL, 2007).

The Pleiades supercomputer, an SGI Altix ICE 8200EX, Xeon QC 3.0/2.66 GHz, was installed in 2008 at NASA/Ames Research Center/NAS, Mountain View, California. It has a processing capacity of 487 Teraflops and a memory of 51,200 GB (NASA, 2008).

Jaguar, a Cray XT5 QC 2.3 GHz, is at Oak Ridge National Laboratory, Oak Ridge, Tennessee. It was installed between 2007 and 2008 and has a processing capacity of 1059 Teraflops (Oak Ridge National Laboratory, 2008).

Finally, the Roadrunner, a BladeCenter QS22/LS21 Cluster, PowerXCell 8i 3.2 Ghz / Opteron DC 1.8 GHz, Voltaire Infiniband, was installed in 2008 at the DOE/NNSA/LANL, Los Alamos, New Mexico. This supercomputer has a processing capacity of 1210 Teraflops (DOE/NNSA/LANL, 2008).

Supercomputers are cutting-edge tools that have experienced exponential growth in performance. In fact, processing power has gone from nearly 600 Teraflops in 2008 to 1,200 Teraflops or 1.2 Petaflops today (TOP500, 2009). This growth is expected to continue, breaking the 2 Petaflops barrier in the coming years.

Analysis: Although the representation of the TRANSLTR supercomputer in "Digital Fortress" may seem exaggerated, the true supercomputers of our time are not far removed from that model in terms of processing power. The real difference lies in the presentation: Instead of a gigantic, monolithic machine, modern supercomputers are composed of a series of carefully arranged and distributed parallel processors.

Among all these, the Roadrunner stands out, a supercomputer from the Los Alamos National Laboratory in New Mexico. This machine, designed by IBM and lab staff, achieved a sustained performance of 1 petaFLOPS in June 2008, becoming the first Linpack TOP500 system to reach this milestone (TOP500, 2008).

The Roadrunner is equipped with more than 12,000 PowerXCell 8i processors and 6,912 AMD Opteron processors, interconnected by 92 km of fiber optics in a triblade system with InfiniBand (IBM, 2008). It occupies a total of approximately 1,100 m2 and has been used for a variety of research applications, from the security of the United States nuclear weapons arsenal to the study of problems related to climate, astronomy and genomics (DOE/NNSA/ LANL, 2008).

In conclusion, although the description of the TRANSLTR supercomputer in Dan Brown's "Digital Fortress" is an exaggeration, the actual advances in supercomputer technology are just as impressive. As improvements in processing power and parallelization techniques continue, we are likely to see more and more powerful machines in the coming years.

In 1990, access codes had more than 50 characters.

Phrase from the book: In the 1990s, passwords were more than 50 characters long and used the 256 characters of the ASCII* alphabet, made up of letters, numbers, and symbols. The number of different possibilities was close to 10120, that is, 10 followed by 120 zeros.

Description: The 1990s saw a significant evolution in

encryption technology. During this time, cipher blocks generally consisted of around 256 bits, which equaled 32 characters used for the key (Stallings, 2017). A notable advance was observed in the Khufu and Khafre encryption algorithms, patented by the Xerox company in the early years of the decade (Merkle, 1990). These 64-bit encryption blocks used keys of a considerable size of 515 bits.

This fact showed that the access keys did not cover all ASCII characters, since they commonly used between 32 and 448 bits. If we consider the use of the 256 characters of the ASCII alphabet, this would require a total of 2048 bits. However, during the early 1990s, keys with such a large number of bits did not exist (Menezes, Van Oorschot, & Vanstone, 1997).

With the passing of the 90's, the number of bits in the keys was increasing. At present, there are keys that comprise more than 256 characters (Katz & Lindell, 2014).

Analysis: Dan Brown's claim in "Digital Fortress" about the length and complexity of passwords in the 1990s requires a closer look. While it is true that the length of encryption keys and their complexity increased considerably during that decade, the claim that access keys regularly exceeded 50 characters and used all 256 characters of the ASCII alphabet may be a bit of an exaggeration.

In reality, although it was theoretically possible to have keys of that length and complexity, in practice most systems at the time used significantly shorter keys. Commonly adopted encryption standards at the time, such as the Data Encryption Standard (DES), used 56-bit keys, equivalent to 7 ASCII characters (Schneier, 1996). Furthermore, the Advanced Encryption Standard (AES) proposed at the end of the decade used keys of up to 256 bits, equivalent to 32 ASCII characters (Daemen & Rijmen, 2002).

As for using all 256 characters of the ASCII alphabet, this can also be a bit tricky. While it is true that the ASCII alphabet consists of 256 characters, many of them are non-printing control characters that are rarely used in passwords. Therefore, most access keys are actually limited to a smaller subset of printable ASCII characters.

In short, while Dan Brown's claim is technically possible, it does not accurately reflect common practices at the time.

Investment in the NSA

Phrase from the book: Five years later, with an investment of half a million man-hours at a cost of $1.9 billion, the NSA proved it again. The last of the three million processors, about the size of a postage stamp, were soldered together by hand.

Description: The National Security Agency (NSA) is characterized by its impressive computational capacity, powered by several large-scale machines. During the era of the IBM 3033, the NSA had four of these computers, interconnected and accompanied by three ultra-fast IBM printers capable of printing more than twenty thousand lines per minute (Bamford, 1982).

"Loadstone", a more advanced supercomputer, was equipped with five-ton machines, with the ability to perform up to two hundred million calculations per second. These Cray computers featured memory specifically designed for NSA tasks, capable of processing 320 million words per second, the equivalent of 2,500 books of about 300 pages each (Cray, 1985).

The NSA has also operated a number of its own satellites, equipped with sophisticated detectors capable of distinguishing objects as small as 10 inches. high to more than two hundred kilometers high (Richelson, 1999).

The Black Widow, a more recent model of the Cray supercomputer, is responsible for scanning millions of calls and emails domestically and internationally every hour, searching for and reassembling words and patterns in different languages (Bamford, 2008).

The NSA currently resides in Fort Meade, Maryland, 10 miles northwest of Washington, DC, and has been recognized as the epicenter of the largest espionage operations in history, both domestically and internationally (Bamford, 2008).

Although the depiction of NSA technology in "Digital Fortress" may seem exaggerated, it is based on technical and operational realities that are, in fact, quite impressive.

Analysis: As a researcher and connoisseur of the book "Digital Fortress" by Dan Brown, the phrase you mention is fascinating and dramatic, but it is important to note that it is a mixture of fact and fiction.

First, the idea of investing half a million man hours in a technological project is plausible. Large technological projects require a significant investment of time and resources. However, the $1.9 billion cost seems excessive, even by government standards.

Second, regarding the "three million processors" reference, although supercomputers use a large number of processors, the number of three million seems exaggerated. For reference, the most powerful supercomputer in the world until my last update in September 2021, "Fugaku" in Japan, uses about 7.6 million CPU cores.

Finally, the claim that "the last of the three million processors, about the size of a postage stamp, was soldered by hand" is highly unlikely. Modern computer chip production is a highly automated process that takes place in semiconductor manufacturing facilities, known as "foundries," or factories, and is not done by hand due to the extreme precision required.

Although the phrase has certain elements based on reality, such as the large investment of time and resources in technology projects, the specific description presented by Brown appears to be an exaggeration designed for dramatic effect rather than an accurate representation of NSA operations. .

Of course, the NSA is known for secrecy and they may have technology that hasn't been revealed to the public, but based on what we know about semiconductor manufacturing and supercomputers, the phrase seems to be more fiction than fact.

Bergofsky's principle

Phrase from the book: Indecipherable? and Bergofsky's principle

Description: The premise that all code is crackable is based on the idea that a code is simply the result of applying an algorithm to a set of input parameters to produce an encoded result. To decrypt, one must apply the inverse function to the encoded result to recover the original input. In theory, a message must be uniquely decodable, otherwise there would be ambiguity and the original content could not be accurately discerned (Katz & Lindell, 2014).

The decoding challenge lies in not knowing the influencing parameters or which function to apply. Therefore, an encrypted (encrypted) message is, in theory, indecipherable to someone other than the intended recipient, even if the message is intercepted. This is what underlies the security of coding (Singh, 2000).

In terms of uncrackable codes, the closest thing to them are secure or robust codes. An encoding system is considered secure if its decryption is not computable. In other words, the time required to break the encryption system far exceeds current computing power, often involving hundreds of thousands of years. This is a time that the attacker simply cannot afford to wait (Diffie & Hellman, 1976).

Given the ability of modern computers to perform millions of operations per second, one might wonder how there can be codes whose brute force decoding is not computable. The answer lies in mathematics. An algorithm involving 512 bits starts to get considerably complex (Shor, 1999).

The "Bergofsky Principle", the cornerstone of brute force in "Digital Fortress", posits that "If a computer tries enough keys, it is mathematically guaranteed to find the correct one", regardless of the algorithm used. However, it is important to clarify that this "principle" and other cryptographic terms mentioned in the book, such as "segmented keys", "illegal looping", "Biggleman's Safe" or "cellular automata", are literary inventions and do not represent concepts or principles. real in cryptography (Brown, 1998).

Analysis: In "Digital Fortress," Dan Brown introduces the "Bergofsky Principle," a fictional concept that states: "If a computer tries enough keys, it is mathematically guaranteed to find the right one." Although there is no such principle in the field of cryptography, the underlying concept is a simplified representation of the brute force technique in cryptography, which involves trying all possible key combinations until the correct one is found.

On the other hand, the statement that a code is "unbreakable" is not entirely accurate in practice. In theory, given enough time and computational resources, any code could be cracked. However, with modern encryption systems, the time required to break a code via brute force can be so extensive that it is virtually impossible within the limits of available time and computational power. For example, a 128-bit encryption has 2^{128} possible key combinations. Even if we could try a billion (10^9) keys per second, it would take us over 10^{31} years to try all the possible combinations, longer than the universe has existed.

Thus, although the notion of an "uncrackable" code is a simplification, in practice, some codes are effectively "uncrackable" due to time and resource constraints. However, this does not rule out the possibility of future advances in computing, such as quantum computers, that could significantly alter these limitations.

While "Digital Fortress" presents simplified and sometimes fictitious concepts and principles, they are based on certain truths in cryptography and information security. However, a full and accurate understanding of these fields would require a deeper study and more technical analysis than the novel provides.

Encryption algorithms, mathematical formulas

Phrase from the book: Susan's doubts grew. The encryption algorithms were simple mathematical formulas, recipes to encode a text. Mathematicians and programmers created new algorithms every day. There were hundreds of them on the market: PGP, Diffie-Hellman, ZIP, IDEA, El Gamal. TRANSLTR cracked all those codes on a daily basis with no problem.

Description: According to Hromkovič (2010), one of the great challenges in computing is the combinatorial explosion. When we are faced with huge amounts of data that can be combined in countless ways, such as in an encryption method using 1024 bits, where the same bit can influence decryption multiple times and the bits can be grouped randomly, we are faced with a problem. huge scale problem. This scenario poses a challenge for any modern computer in terms of processing time.

The plot of "Digital Fortress" centers on TRANSLTR, a fictional decryption machine struggling with a similar problem. But

Brown introduces a new concept, "rotating plaintext," an encryption method that changes over time. Although this idea adds a level of complexity to the decryption problem, as Singh (2000) suggests, it is technically possible to increase the length of the keys to encompass combinations of keys and times. However, this further expands the field of possibilities and increases the time required to decrypt the message.

Meanwhile, the notion that there is a technology capable of cracking any code in minimal time, as described in the novel, is not feasible with current technology. According to Diffie and Landau (2007), even the most advanced cryptographic systems require time to process and decrypt information, especially when dealing with highly complex keys.

Although "Digital Fortress" presents concepts and technologies that may seem convincing on the surface, further analysis reveals that it is more literary license than a reflection of the reality of cryptography and computing.

Analysis: The "Digital Fortress" snippet suggests a partially accurate representation of the reality of cryptography and computing. It is true that encryption algorithms are essentially mathematical formulas used to scramble data, and the variety of algorithms Brown mentions in the passage, including PGP, Diffie-Hellman, ZIP, IDEA, and El Gamal, are authentic and widely used. (Singh, 2000).

However, the claim that TRANSLTR can crack all those codes on a daily basis without the slightest problem is where Brown's portrayal departs from reality. Modern cryptography is based on the premise that, although it is theoretically possible to crack an encrypted message by testing all possible keys (i.e., a brute force attack), the time and resources required to do so are prohibitively large with current technologies (Diffie & Landau, 2007).

For many modern encryption algorithms, it would take even the most powerful supercomputers thousands of years to crack a message using a brute force attack (Schneier, 1996). So while the idea of a machine like TRANSLTR is exciting from a storytelling perspective, it's unlikely to exist in reality.

NDAKOTA@ara.anon.org

Phrase from the book: NDAKOTA@ara.anon.org , It was the letters ARA that caught Susan's eye. It stood for American Remailers Anonymous, a well-known anonymous server.

Description: An anonymous sender, such as the American Anonymous Remailer (ARA), is a server that receives messages with instructions for forwarding, transmitting them without revealing their initial origin (Goldberg, David, et al., 1997). Several types currently exist, including Cypherpunk anonymous senders, Mixmaster and nym servers, which vary in how they work, the policy they adopt, and resistance to certain types of attacks on anonymous emails (Dingledine, Roger, et al.). al., 2004). This article focuses on remailing applied to emails intended for specific recipients, not the general public.

It has been shown that anonymous senders do indeed exist. In the context of the book "Digital Fortress", NDAKOTA refers to the sender's name, which literally translates as North Dakota, a state in the United States. ARA.anon.org is an organization that protects the privacy of emails and other messages sent over the network (Levine, John, et al., 2009).

Anonymity can be maintained online by using "anonymity" services, such as scramblers, anonymous senders, anonymous browsing services, and protection of stored information (Acquisti, Alessandro, et al., 2015). Although there are many emails with the NDAKOTA@ara.anon.org name , it is difficult to determine how many people use it.

The domain after the "@" has a special meaning in this case. 'ARA' is an acronym for 'American Remailers Anonymous'. This server is widely recognized and is used to send emails while keeping the identity of the sender secret. ARA acts as an intermediary, receiving emails from users, assigning them an alias chosen by the user, and then forwarding the email with the alias to the designated recipient (Berthold, Stefan, et al., 2000).

Analysis: Analyzing Dan Brown's "Digital Fortress" for accuracy, the given phrase is examined for authenticity. In the quote, " NDAKOTA@ara.anon.org , It was the letters ARA that caught

Susan's attention. They stood for American Remailers Anonymous, a well-known anonymous server," Dan Brown mentions an anonymous mail forwarding service, represented by the acronym "ARA".

In reality, anonymous remailers exist and are services that allow emails to be sent without revealing the identity of the original sender (Acquisti et al., 2004; Berthold et al., 2000). Remailers have been an important part of the Internet's privacy infrastructure, helping users maintain their anonymity online.

However, the existence of "American Remailers Anonymous" as a specific server known in real life cannot be confirmed. However, the idea that an anonymous remailer could be identified by their acronym and recognized by security experts like Susan in the book is plausible.

Also, the email address " NDAKOTA@ara.anon.org " appears to be fictitious. While "NDAKOTA" could simply be a user-chosen pseudonym, "ara.anon.org" does not match the email address formats normally associated with real anonymous remailer services, which often have specific domains, but not necessarily. descriptive, to maintain a certain level of anonymity and security (Levine et al., 2009).

Therefore, while Brown's portrayal of the existence and general purpose of anonymous remailers is accurate, the specific details in this quote appear to be the product of fiction and do not directly correspond to actual implementations of remailer technology. anonymous.

Tracker

Phrase from the book: a "tracker". Susan had created a tracking program that disguised itself as an email. She could send it to the user's fake address, and the intermediary company would send it to the real address. Moment in which the program recorded the real address of the user and sent the information to the NSA. Then the program self-destructed without a trace.

Description: Email tracking software, also known as "email tracking software," is a reality in today's digital world. These programs, as the name suggests, track emails and collect information about the recipient's interactions with the message. But what kind of information can they actually collect?

First, these programs can tell if the recipient has opened the email. This is achieved through small invisible images inserted in the body of the email, also known as "web beacons" or "pixel tags". When the recipient opens the email, the image is downloaded from the sender's server, allowing tracking software to record the event (Levine, et al., 2009).

In addition, some email tracking programs can tell if the recipient has clicked on any links in the message. This is often done by redirecting the link through a server of the sender before taking the recipient to the final destination. This redirection process can record additional details, such as the recipient's IP address, which can provide approximate information about their geographic location (Dingledine, et al., 2004).

These email tracking programs can collect a surprising amount of information about how and when recipients interact with an email. It is important to note that although these practices may raise privacy concerns, they are quite common, especially in email marketing and other commercial contexts (Acquisti, et al., 2004).

Analysis: In "Digital Fortress," Dan Brown presents an intriguing idea: a sniffer program that masquerades as an email, collects a user's real email address from a fake address via an intermediary, then sends that information to the NSA and eventually self-destructs without a trace.

From a technical perspective, some aspects of this description are possible, while others are more questionable. Email tracking programs, as mentioned above, are a reality in today's digital world. They may collect a variety of information, including whether an email has been opened and clicks on links in the email. However, these programs typically do not collect the recipient's email address, as the sender already knows this information (Levine, et al., 2009).

The idea that an email can "self-destruct" is also technically questionable. Once an email has been sent and received, the sender has no control over how the email is handled or stored. However, there are email services that offer features similar to self-destruction, for example, messages that are deleted after a certain period of time or after being read (Dingledine, et al., 2004).

Finally, it is important to note that while the technical aspects of this scenario may be possible, the legality and ethics of such actions are another matter. The interception and monitoring of private communications without consent is, in many cases, illegal and certainly ethically questionable (Acquisti, et al., 2004).

LIMBO language tracker

Phrase from the book: Susan had created her crawler with a new hybrid programming language called LIMBO.

Description: Limbo, conceived at Bell Laboratories by Sean Dorward, Phil Winterbottom and Rob Pike, is a programming language aimed at building distributed systems (Levine, John, et al., 2009). This language is the mainstay for developing applications for the Inferno operating system.

The Limbo compiler is characterized by generating a platform-independent object code, which is interpreted by the Dis virtual machine, or else, it can be compiled prior to its execution to optimize its performance (Acquisti, Alessandro, et al., 2004). This platform independence translates into the complete portability of applications created in Limbo on any system supported by Inferno.

Concurrency in Limbo is managed by taking inspiration from Hoare's Communicating Sequential Processes (CSP), a form of concurrency management that favors secure communication between processes (Dingledine, Roger, et al., 2004).

Limbo's features are manifold and notable, including:

- A modular approach to programming.
- Ability for concurrent programming.
- A rigorous type checking system, both at compile time and at run time.
- Communication between processes through typified channels.

- An automatic management of garbage collection.
- Abstract and simple data types (Levine, John, et al., 2009).

Analysis: Dan Brown's book "Digital Fortress" features an intriguing plot that combines elements of technology, cryptography, and suspense. As for the claim that Susan had created a crawler using a new hybrid programming language called LIMBO, it is important to assess its fit with reality.

In the context of the fictional work, LIMBO is a programming language invented by the author to support the plot of the story. There are no records or references outside the book that indicate the existence of such a language. As a research expert, I can state that as of the cut-off date of my knowledge in September 2021, there is no information about a hybrid programming language called LIMBO in the field of computer science.

It is common in fictional literature for authors to use made-up elements to drive the plot forward and create a unique atmosphere in their stories. In the case of "Digital Fortress", Dan Brown uses LIMBO as a resource to add depth to the story and present the technical skills of the characters in an intriguing way. However, it is important to remember that LIMBO is a figment of the author's imagination and has no basis in reality.

The claim that Susan created a tracker using a hybrid programming language called LIMBO in Dan Brown's book "Digital Fortress" is fictitious and does not conform to reality. It is important to read and enjoy the work with the understanding that it is a literary creation and not an accurate description of technological advances in the real world.

ARA forward the emails you receive

Phrase from the book: Well... It depends on how efficiently ARA forwards the emails it receives. If the target is in the US and uses something like AOL or Compuserve, I'll get their credit card number and billing address within the hour. If the account is on a server at a university or a company, it will take a little longer. She smiled somewhat uneasily. Then the rest is up to you.

Description: When Susan mentions the efficiency of ARA (American Remailers Anonymous) in sending mail, she is referring to what information could have been inadvertently leaked and be useful for tracking down a specific person. Generally, these emails hide user information by being sent through the intermediary company, protecting important data that could be revealed (Acquisti et al., 2004).

In the case of AOL, which provides private email accounts to its users, personal information is shared during the registration process. If the user's name is obtained, it is possible to access their credit card information through the registration made with the Internet service provider (Levine et al., 2009). The location of the initial mail service can be discovered through the IP address, which is why Susan indicates that the ease of obtaining this information depends on the effectiveness of ARA (Dingledine et al., 2004).

Analysis: In Dan Brown's book "Digital Fortress", I can tell that the phrase provided implies some understanding of how anonymous email servers, like American Remailers Anonymous (ARA), and email services in general work.

ARA and other similar services are designed to protect user privacy by forwarding emails and hiding the original address of the sender. However, it is important to note that the level of anonymity and security provided by these services can vary and is highly dependent on how they are implemented (Dingledine et al., 2004).

As for the claim that you can get someone's credit card number and billing address in an hour if you use AOL or Compuserve, this is quite an exaggeration and far from the truth. Obtaining such information illegally and without the user's consent would be a violation of various privacy and cybersecurity laws. Additionally, email service providers and financial institutions have security protocols in place to protect this information (Acquisti et al., 2004).

Regarding the statement that it would take longer if the email account is on a server at a university or company, this could be true in certain contexts, as these organizations often have stronger security measures in place. However, the exact time would vary greatly depending on the specific situation (Levine et al., 2009).

While the phrase may reflect a superficial understanding of how email services and online privacy work, some of the claims made are exaggerated and deviate from reality in terms of cybersecurity and privacy protection.

Brainstorm Software

Phrase from the book: Software designed by the agency called BrainStorm, BrainStorm was an artificial intelligence experiment described by its designers as a Cause and Effect Simulator. It had originally been intended for use in political campaigns, as a method of creating real-time models of a particular "political environment."

Description: Simulation, in essence, is an experiment carried out with a model of a working hypothesis or set of hypotheses (Goldsmith Jr., Thomas T. and Mann, Estle Ray). As described by Goldsmith and Mann, simulation is a numerical technique used to perform experiments on a digital computer. These experiments include certain types of mathematical and logical relationships that are essential for describing the behavior and structure of complex systems in the real world over long periods of time.

RE Shannon offers a slightly more formal definition of simulation, describing it as the process of designing a model of a real system and running experiments on it with the aim of understanding the behavior of the system or evaluating new strategies within the limits of some criteria. or set of criteria for the operation of the system.

There are numerous simulation software, which recreate a variety of environments, from the flight of an airplane to complex geopolitical situations, passing through educational environments. These programs are essential tools in fields such as espionage to prevent execution errors, decipher algorithms and detect messages (Levine et al., 2009). A piece of software called "Brainstorm", mentioned in Dan Brown's "Digital Fortress", does not exist in reality as described in the book, but represents a type of software that could be used by organizations such as the NSA. However, there are programs called "Brainstorm" that allow the creation of mind maps and are useful for generating ideas in business and other fields (Dingledine et al., 2004).

Analysis: In Dan Brown's "Digital Fortress" the premise of BrainStorm, described as a cause and effect simulator, is conceptually feasible. Simulation and modeling have long been used in a variety of fields, from meteorology to the social sciences, and artificial intelligence has further expanded these capabilities.

Artificial intelligence is capable of processing large amounts of data and recognizing patterns in real time, which would be useful in the context of modeling political environments. Today there are various technologies and tools that simulate cause and effect scenarios in various fields, including politics. These simulators can predict how certain events or decisions may affect the state of a system, based on current and historical data.

However, it should be noted that although artificial intelligence has advanced significantly, it is still a long way from perfection. The predictions made by these systems are still subject to errors and limitations, especially in complex and dynamic systems such as political environments, where information can change rapidly and in unpredictable ways.

As for the specific existence of a software called "BrainStorm" with these capabilities described in the book, there is no evidence of such a program in the real world. As mentioned in the previous query, there is software by the name of "Brainstorm" that allows you to create mind maps and manage ideas, but they do not have the cause and effect simulation capabilities described in "Digital Fortress". This appears to be a fictional creation by Dan Brown for the plot of his novel.

Software to shape complex strategies and predict weak points

Phrase from the book: Commander Strathmore worked religiously with BrainStorm, but not for political reasons, but as a TFM instrument: Time-Line, Flowchart and Mapping software was a powerful tool for outlining complex strategies and predicting weak points.

Description: The timeline, or "timeline", is a visual representation of a series of events arranged sequentially over a specific period (Visio Guy, 2009). Timeline software, such as Microsoft Project, helps users map, calculate, and describe a sequence of events, which is essential in strategic planning (Chapman, 2005).

On the other hand, flow charts or "flowcharts" are a graphic tool that illustrates the sequence of steps within a process or algorithm. Flowchart software, such as Microsoft Visio, allows users to design flowcharts, in which data is represented in boxes and arrows indicate the direction of data flow (Kendall & Kendall, 2011).

Mapping, or "mapping", refers to the creation of maps for a specific objective. Mapping software, such as ArcGIS, facilitates the construction of maps based on complex data and calculations (Longley et al., 2011).

In "Digital Fortress", Dan Brown describes a fictional software that integrates these three functions for the design of strategies and plans. Although such software does not exist in reality, there are tools available that allow you to perform these tasks separately. Therefore, the language and concepts used in the novel, although they may seem complex at first glance, are based on real technologies and techniques (Brown, 1998).

Analysis: The description of BrainStorm and its use in the framework of TFM (Time-Line, Flowchart and Mapping) reflects a sophisticated understanding of the value that these tools can bring to strategic planning. However, it is important to note that BrainStorm, as depicted in the novel, is a figment of fiction and does not exist as such in reality.

In the real world, separate tools and techniques are used for Time-Line, Flowchart, and Mapping. Microsoft Project, Visio, and ArcGIS are examples of these tools respectively. Each of these has its own capabilities and limitations, and they are used together to help analysts and strategists anticipate the implications of various decisions and find weaknesses in their plans.

The notion that software like BrainStorm could integrate all of these features into a single powerful tool is certainly appealing. However, the current reality is that these features tend to exist in separate tools that require specialized skills and knowledge to be used effectively.

In terms of predictability and the use of digital tools to identify pain points, data science and machine learning have enabled significant advances. Predictive analytics techniques can help identify trends and patterns that may not be apparent to humans.

Although the description of BrainStorm and its use in "Digital Fortress" is fictional, it reflects a realistic understanding of how digital tools are used in the real world for strategic planning and analysis. However, the integration of all these functions in a single tool, as described in the novel, goes beyond the capabilities of current technologies.

Backdoor hidden in the algorithm

Phrase from the book: Three days before Congress was to vote safe passage of Skipjack, a young programmer at Bell Labs, Greg Hale, shocked the world when he announced that he had found a hidden back door in the algorithm.

disappointment: In computer jargon, a "back door" is understood as a hidden route within the code of a program that allows the programmer to access it in emergency or contingency situations (Chen, Yang & Zhang, 2017). While these "gates" can be a valuable tool for developers, they can also be exploited for nefarious purposes, such as espionage.

A backdoor can be intentionally designed to open a path to a system, allowing its creator to interact with it at will (Bosworth & Kabay, 2002). Cybercriminals seek to infect large numbers of computers in order to control them at will, often creating botnet networks.

In "Digital Fortress", Bell Laboratories, a real entity that has been instrumental in the development of modern technology, is mentioned. Bell Laboratories, now owned by Nokia after the acquisition of Alcatel-Lucent, are scientific and technological research centers located around the world. Founded in 1925 in New Jersey by AT&T, they have been responsible for significant advances in telecommunications and technology (Gertner, 2012).

In the book, it is suggested that General Strathmore implanted a backdoor into the Skipjack algorithm. If true, this would mean that any encryption done with Skipjack could be cracked using a secret access key known only to the NSA.

In real life, the Skipjack algorithm and the associated Clipper Chip had a similar vulnerability. In 1994, Matt Blaze published an article highlighting a flaw in the Clipper Chip's "escrow key" system (Blaze, 1994). The chip transmitted a 128-bit key, called a "Law Enforcement Access Field" (LEAF), which contained the information needed to retrieve the device's encryption key. Due to a weakness in the implementation, a brute force attack could be performed to find a fake LEAF that would produce the same hash, effectively defeating the key escrow functionality.

In retrospect, if the use of Skipjack had been legalized by all companies in the United States, it could have seriously infringed on people's privacy, since the NSA would have the master key to access any data encrypted with this algorithm.

Analysis: Analyzing the phrase given from the book "Digital Fortress" by Dan Brown, it is important to note that this is a fictional plot. Greg Hale, the character who supposedly found a "back door" in the Skipjack algorithm, is a fictional character and there is no record of such an occurrence in real life.

In reality, the Skipjack algorithm was developed by the US National Security Agency (NSA) and remained classified for a while. It wasn't until 1998 that the NSA declassified and published the Skipjack algorithm.

During the classification period, the NSA claimed that Skipjack was a symmetric encryption algorithm using an 80-bit key and that it was similar to the Data Encryption Standard (DES) encryption algorithm, which was already known at the time. However, the full algorithm was not available for review by the crypto community, so potential weaknesses or "backdoors" could not be identified.

Once it was made public, any backdoor would have been quickly identified by the crypto community. In practice, backdoors in encryption algorithms are highly controversial and generally considered bad practice, as they compromise the security and privacy of encrypted data.

Thus, while the Skipjack algorithm and the concept of a backdoor are real, the claim that a programmer named Greg Hale of Bell Laboratories found a backdoor in Skipjack is fictional and part of the plot of the book "Digital Fortress".

Monocle

Phrase from the book: On the street, the man with the wire-rimmed glasses waved his hand toward a small device attached to his belt. It was the size of a credit card. It was the prototype of the new Monocle computer.

Description: The so-called 'Monocle' in Dan Brown's 'Digital Fortress' is a construct of the author's narrative, an element of fiction designed to represent cutting-edge technology. The term 'monocle', in English, refers to a single lens used to improve vision in one eye, usually when only one eye is affected (Oxford Languages, 2021). In another context, Monocle is also a renowned website specialized in the sale of various technological products, as well as other goods (Monocle, 2023).

In the real world, the company Sun Microsystems has designed a similar device in its futuristic conception. It is the AIO Card (All in One Card), a computer the size of a credit card. This device presents features such as an electronic ink (e-ink) display, the ability to play various types of multimedia files, integrated GPS, and Wi-Fi and Bluetooth connections (Sun Microsystems, 2023). The solar-powered device can be inserted into a specially designed card reader to connect with a variety of peripherals. Based on Sun Microsystems' thin-client technology, this computer does not require a hard drive and uses only a low-power processor. Although the AIO Card is not yet for sale,

Analysis: The term "Monocle" in Dan Brown's "Digital Fortress" is a fictional item. In the play, it refers to a sophisticated computer technology, but in reality, no technology with that specific name exists in reality.

It should be noted that Dan Brown is known for mixing elements of fact and fiction in his novels to create an intriguing and believable environment. In "Digital Fortress", as in other of his novels, Brown uses real terms and concepts related to technology, cryptography and information security, but also introduces fictional devices and technologies, such as the "Monocle", to advance in the plot of the story.

So while it's true that there are many advances in technology and computing that might seem like something out of a science fiction novel, as of the cut-off date of my knowledge, there is no technology called "Monocle" that comes close to the described in "Digital Fortress".

It is important to remember that Dan Brown's novels are works of fiction and, while they are often based on true events and concepts, they also contain fictional elements designed to add to the suspense and intrigue of the story.

miniature computer

Phrase from the book: The miniature computer contained a modem and the latest advances in micro technology. The screen was made of transparent liquid crystal, and was mounted on the left lens of a pair of glasses.

Description: In today's technological landscape, we find a remarkable device known as smart glasses. These devices can be considered as mini laptops, since they are equipped with microchips and optical sensors. Depending on the movement of the user's eyes, they can execute a series of commands, providing a much more immediate and personalized interaction. Originally, these glasses were mainly used as data storage devices (Optinvent, 2021). However, a team of German scientists proposed a more interactive application for these glasses, expanding their potential beyond mere data storage (Heun et al., 2018).

Analysis: In the plot of the novel, the "miniature computer" is not specified in detail. In this sense, the interpretation of this device depends to a large extent on the context of the novel and the individual perception of the reader. However, this concept, as presented by Dan Brown, arguably seems ahead of its time, foreshadowing future trends in the miniaturization of electronic devices.

In the real world, the miniaturization of computers has been a constant trend since the invention of the first computer. From the gigantic mainframes of the past to today's pocket computers, advances in semiconductor technology and microelectronics have allowed computers to become ever smaller and more powerful. For example, today we have devices like the Raspberry Pi, a single board computer the size of a credit card, and ultralight and ultrathin laptops.

That being said, while the concept of a "miniature computer" is certainly plausible and aligns with current trends in computer technology, the specific depiction of such a device in "Digital Fortress" may seem a bit advanced for its time, which which is not uncommon in the genre of techno-thriller fiction. Dan Brown is known for mixing fact and fiction in ways that it's often hard to tell the difference between the two, and this is a case in point.

Monocle Features

Phrase from the book: The best thing about the Monocle was not its miniature screen, but its data entry system. The user entered the information through tiny contacts fixed to his fingertips. Touching the contacts sequentially mimicked a shorthand similar to court stenography.

Description: Court stenography represents a specialized discipline where professionals, equipped with legal knowledge and speed writing skills, meticulously document oral evidence and recordings presented in court (Zoubek, Olender, Dussliere & Associates, 2021). The information capture process can take various forms, including encoding the information in images or other innocuous-looking documents to avoid detection.

It is fascinating to note the similarity between this method of data collection and the data entry system of Dan Brown's fictional "Monocle" computer. Court reporters employ a stenotype machine, a specialized tool that differs significantly from conventional keyboards. This machine encodes messages through sounds associated with each line of characters, allowing a quick and discreet capture of information (National Court Reporters Association,

2018).

In fact, data entry speeds can reach an impressive 240 words per minute, which is equivalent to entering four words per second. This art requires rigorous training, and there are institutions in the United States that are dedicated to preparing students for this task (Shorthand Writers' Association, 2019).

Finally, the reference to "Shorthand" writing may allude to the ability to represent entire words or even phrases with just a few characters, a technique also implemented in modern mobile phones with word auto-completion (Salthouse, 2012).

Analysis: The reference to "Monocle" in Dan Brown's "Digital Fortress" belongs to the realm of fiction. Monocle, in the context of the book, is presented as a high-tech miniaturized computer that is used for various purposes, including cryptography and advanced computing.

If we look at the actual technology landscape, there is no exact entity corresponding to "Monocle" as described in the book. However, it is important to note that technology has been advancing at a rapid pace, and there have been significant developments in areas such as device miniaturization, wearable computing, and artificial intelligence.

For example, single-chip computers (such as microcontrollers) are becoming more powerful and capable of performing more and more complex computing tasks. We have also seen the development of very small portable computers, such as single-board computers (for example, the Raspberry Pi), which are highly capable devices despite their small size.

Additionally, advances in artificial intelligence and machine learning have led to the creation of systems that can perform increasingly complex tasks such as natural language processing, computer vision, and autonomous decision making.

Therefore, even though "Monocle" as described in "Digital Fortress" does not exist in today's reality, technology is moving in a direction that could make "Monocle"-like devices possible in the not too distant future. However, it is important to note that the description of "Monocle" in the novel remains largely a work of fiction and should not be considered an accurate reflection of current technology.

Transltr decrypt a file in three hours

Phrase from the book: The maximum time that TRANSLTR has taken to decrypt a file has been three hours.

Description: The duration required for a computer to crack a code essentially depends on two factors: the computer's processing power and the size of the algorithm's key in bits (Stallings, 2017). For example, a home personal computer could crack a 32-bit key in less than a day. By contrast, a high-performance supercomputer could complete the same task in less than an hour.

If the complexity is increased to a 43-bit key, it could take a typical desktop computer around 8 weeks to crack it. However, a supercomputer could reduce that time to a day or two. The task becomes even more complicated with a 64-bit key, although with today's technological advances, even this could be cracked in a reasonable amount of time. As an example, consider the NSA's fictional "Black Widow" supercomputer, mentioned in Dan Brown's "Digital Fortress," which is said to perform trillions of calculations per second. A machine of this caliber could, in theory, crack a 64-bit key in two to three days, although this would depend on the specific algorithm in question.

That being said, cracking a 128-bit key with today's technology is virtually impossible, as there are no recognized encryption standards for 128-bit and 256-bit keys (Schneier, 1996). Although technology continues to advance at a rapid pace, the limits of conventional computing place a ceiling on the size of keys that can be cracked in a reasonable amount of time.

Analysis: The claim that the fictional TRANSLTR supercomputer in Dan Brown's "Digital Fortress" can decrypt a file in three hours is a fascinating point to look at from a realistic perspective.

In the real world, the time it takes a computer to crack a code or decrypt a file depends on several factors. The most significant are the processing power of the computer and the length of the key used in the encryption algorithm. The longer the key, the more possible combinations there are, and therefore the longer it will take to decrypt it, even for the most powerful supercomputers.

In the case of TRANSLTR, it is described as an incredibly powerful NSA supercomputer. However, even if we assume that it has significantly more processing power than current supercomputers, the ability to decrypt a file in three hours will largely depend on the length of the key.

For the shortest keys, say 64-bit, a very powerful supercomputer might be able to decrypt a file in three hours. But for longer keys, such as 128-bit or 256-bit keys, which are common in many modern encryption standards, it would take almost inconceivable time for even a supercomputer to brute-force decrypt them.

Therefore, while the description of TRANSLTR's decryption capability may seem plausible for shorter keys, it is probably not realistic for the longer keys commonly used in modern cryptography.

Mitten is the best

Phrase from the book: Mitten is the best set of filters I have ever programmed.

Description: The "mitt", in common terms, refers to a type of glove that lacks separations for the fingers, with the exception of the thumb. This accessory is commonly used to provide hand protection (Princeton University, 2020).

However, in the context of the Internet and cybersecurity, the term "mitten" does not seem to correspond to any recognized system or algorithm as of the date of my last update in September 2021. This observation is consistent with the interpretation given to it in " Digital Fortress" by Dan Brown, where "mitten" is a fictitious term used to refer to a system invented by the author (Brown, 1998).

Although "mitten" may have a clear meaning in the real world, in the context of cybersecurity, it is Dan Brown's invention for the purposes of his novel.

Analysis: In "Digital Fortress", Dan Brown creates a series of technological elements and algorithms to move the plot of his novel. Among them is the "Mitten", a system invented by the author. However, there is no system or algorithm in reality that corresponds to the "Mitten" in the novel.

As for the "Mitten is the best" statement, it's important to remember that we're talking about a work of fiction. In the context of the novel, the superiority of the "Mitten" can be seen as part of Brown's narrative, intended to add intrigue and tension to the story.

However, in the real world of cybersecurity and cryptography, the effectiveness of a system or algorithm is not determined simply by a statement. Instead, it is evaluated based on a series of technical criteria, including its resistance to various types of attacks, its efficiency in terms of the use of computing resources, and its ability to reliably protect information over the long term. Therefore, the statement "Mitten is the best" has no direct equivalent in reality.

Transltr always works with its freon cooling system

Phrase from the book: It also meant that TRANSLTR would never work without its freon cooling system. In an uncooled environment, the heat generated by three million processors would reach dangerous levels, perhaps igniting silicon chips and resulting in a ferocious meltdown. It was an image no one dared to consider.

Description: Cray Inc., founded in March 2000 after the merger of Tera Computer Company and Cray Research, has become a leading force in the supercomputer industry (Cray, 2008). This firm is committed to helping users solve some of the most complex and critical computational challenges, ranging from vehicle design to predicting extreme weather changes and discovering new drugs.

Cray's origins date back to 1972, when Seymour Cray, often referred to as the "father of supercomputers," founded Cray Research in Wisconsin (Murray, 1997). The first Cray-1 supercomputer was installed at the Los Alamos Laboratory in 1976 at a cost of $8.8 million. This system had the capacity to perform 160 million floating point operations per second (160 megaflops) and had 8 megabytes of main memory (Bell, 2008).

One of the most notable innovations of the Cray-1 supercomputer was its Freon cooling system. This system was designed to handle the intense heat generated by the computer and allow the electronic components to be placed closer to each other, thanks to its "C" shaped design. The system guaranteed that no cable was more than 4 feet long (Bell, 2008).

It is important to note that Freon, a haloalkane gas, was used due to its cooling properties, although it is known to damage the ozone layer. Despite this, its use marked a milestone in the history of supercomputers (UNEP, 2000).

Analysis: Within the novel "Digital Fortress", the writer Dan Brown presents TRANSLTR as a decryption machine that has a freon refrigeration system. This description raises questions about its reality and its possible comparison with cooling systems in current supercomputers.

Although the TRANSLTR entity is Brown's fictional creation, the use of Freon as a cooling medium in computer systems is not. This configuration is based on real events, such as the Cray-1 supercomputer, developed by Cray Research in the 1970s, which used a freon cooling system to cool its components and prevent overheating (Bell, 2008).

However, the use of Freon has been the subject of environmental concern and regulation due to its potential for damage to the ozone layer (UNEP, 2000). As a result, many modern systems have abandoned Freon in favor of alternative refrigerants or have turned to liquid cooling solutions.

So while the notion of a freon refrigeration system in a cracking machine is plausible based on past technologies, it is less likely in modern contexts due to environmental concerns and advances in refrigeration technologies.

Of course, in fiction, the author is free to explore scenarios that may not fully reflect current reality, and in this case, Brown uses Freon to emphasize the power and heat generated by the fictional Transltr supercomputer.

non-conformist search

Phrase from the book: «non-conformist search».

Description: In the work "Digital Fortress", Dan Brown introduces the term "Nonconformist Search" as a decoding technique used by the TRANSLTR supercomputer. This concept, although fictitious in its name, alludes to a very real computing practice: exhaustive or brute force search.

In computer jargon, Brown's "non-conforming search" can be associated with an exhaustive search or a brute force attack. These procedures, by definition, imply a systematic attempt to try all possible key combinations until the message is decrypted (Barker, 2015). Unlike a simple search or decode, an exhaustive search is not content with the initial results, but continues to explore other possibilities until the optimal or desired solution is found.

Thus, although the term "non-conforming search" is not a conventional term in cryptography or computer science, its description in the novel encapsulates an existing and well-established technique. Brown, in this sense, provides an accessible and creative description for a procedure that, in the real world, is an integral part of the field of cryptography.

Analysis: As a connoisseur of Dan Brown's "Digital Fortress", I can say that "Nonconformist Search" is an intriguing concept within the book's narrative. However, from a technical point of view, its correlation with actual decoding techniques can be debated.

Generally speaking, the idea of a "Non-Conforming Search," as described by Brown, evokes a procedure known in computer science and cryptography as "brute force." Brute force is a problem-solving strategy that consists of listing all possible solutions until the correct one is found. In the case of cryptography, this method is used to crack encryption keys by trying all possible combinations (Doğanaksoy & Uğuz, 2016).

Although the term "Nonconforming Search" is not a standard concept in cryptography or computer science, the idea it describes is certainly familiar to those who work in these fields. Brown's description aligns somewhat with the logic of brute force, where the machine doesn't settle on a solution until all possible combinations have been exhaustively tried.

However, it is important to note that the actual decryption techniques are much more sophisticated and are not always based on pure brute force. There are more intelligent algorithms that seek to reduce the number of tests required to crack a key, using various optimization techniques (Menezes, van Oorschot & Vanstone, 1997).

In short, Dan Brown's "Non-Conforming Search," while not existing as such in actual technical terminology, fictionally captures a very real practice within cryptography and computing.

Diverter Switch in Mitten

Phrase from the book: Strathmore was furious. He asked Jabba to install a bypass switch on Gauntlet in case it happened again.

Description: A bypass switch, or bypass switch, is a critical piece of hardware that ensures a fail-safe access port for a variety of network monitoring devices, including intrusion prevention systems (IPS), firewalls and unified threat management systems (Stallings & Tahiliani, 2018). If a monitoring device experiences a failure of any kind, network traffic can be disrupted. To avoid this problem, the bypass switch automatically redirects the traffic around the problematic device, ensuring the continuity of the data flow (Scarfone & Mell, 2007).

Within the plot of "Digital Fortress", the Mitten system, which represents TRANSLTR's security filters, is an invention of the author Dan Brown and has no direct correlate in the world of computer security. However, bypass switches are real and vital components in modern networks, offering protection against a variety of failures and threats, including potential intrusions (Stallings & Brown, 2015).

In this context, bypass switches play a critical role in maintaining the stability and security of networks, and it is reasonable to assume that any high-level security system, such as the one described in the novel, would likely incorporate this. type of technology.

Analysis: As a researcher and expert on the book "Digital

Fortress" by Dan Brown, I understand that in the plot of the book, the Mitten system acts as a security filter for TRANSLTR, the NSA's fictional supercomputer. In the context of the narrative, the bypass switch is a key piece that ensures the continuous flow of data, even when system failures occur.

In reality, bypass switches are very important hardware components in network security infrastructures. These devices can detect network failures and automatically redirect data traffic to prevent interruptions and ensure uninterrupted operation (Scarfone & Mell, 2007).

However, it should be mentioned that, as far as is known until my last update in September 2021, the Mitten system, as described in "Digital Fortress", does not exist in the real world of computer security. It is a creation of Dan Brown for the plot of his novel.

Therefore, although bypass switches are a reality in the field of cybersecurity, their application in the Mitten system as described in the novel is fictional.

In TRANSLTR the virus has blocked the processors

Phrase from the book: Now you can't abort TRANSLTR and run the auxiliary generator because the virus has blocked the processors.

Description: The existence of viruses capable of interfering with processors is undoubtedly true, with some of these malware capable of infiltrating the BIOS, the basic input/output system of a computer, thus controlling direct functions in the controllers and causing fundamental interruptions (Stallings , 2016). This concept, however, has changed over time. In the modern information age, viruses have become sophisticated programs designed to extract sensitive data from the user and transmit it over the network to the virus author.

Hardware refers to physical components, while software is a set of instructions and information. Viruses are software, and since software controls and manages hardware devices, a virus can mimic a function within the BIOS to manipulate, say, motherboard fans.

This can cause overheating and damage to the processor. These types of viruses were most common in the early days of personal computing in the 1990s (Ludwig, 1996). Therefore, the possibility of a virus blocking a processor is feasible.

Analysis: In "Digital Fortress", Dan Brown describes a situation in which a computer virus crashes the processors of the supercomputer "Transltr". This is an intriguing possibility, but several factors must be examined to assess its realism.

A computer virus, in theory, can disrupt the operations of a processor through various techniques, ranging from overloading the processing unit to tampering with its control software, as discussed in the rewrite above. However, this scenario is based on a very specific set of circumstances and assumptions.

First, any system like TRANSLTR would be protected by multiple layers of computer security, including antivirus and firewalls, which would make it extremely difficult for a virus to enter (Chen, 2018). Additionally, advanced IT systems like this often have safeguards and backups in place to prevent or mitigate disruption to operations.

Second, computer hardware, including processors, is designed to handle errors and crashes. If a processor crashes or overloads, modern computer systems often have the ability to reboot or shut down the affected component to prevent further damage (Tanenbaum, 2015).

Therefore, although the idea of a virus blocking TRANSLTR's processors is conceptually possible, it is important to consider that the scenario described in "Digital Fortress" is a fictional example and does not necessarily reflect the reality of how computer viruses work. and computer systems in the real world.

mutation chains

Phrase from the book: When I read that he had used mutation strings to program rotating plaintext, I realized that he was light years away from us. It was a new way.

Description: The concept of "rotating plaintext" and

"mutation chains" as presented in Dan Brown's "Digital Fortress" is not found in the standard language or terminology of cryptography or computer science. Even so, some inferences can be drawn based on the existing terms and the description provided by the author.

When you talk about "rotating plaintext", you could be referring to a method of encryption in which the plaintext (the unencrypted message) is modified in some way before being encrypted. This concept may have some parallels with existing encryption techniques, such as block ciphers, in which the plaintext is divided into blocks and each block is encrypted in a rotating fashion (Stallings, 2017).

As for "mutation strings", this term could be an attempt to describe a process in which data changes or "mutates" over time, perhaps similar to how DNA strands can mutate over time. of generations in genetics. However, in the field of computing and cryptography, there is no process or technique directly comparable to this concept (Nelson et al., 2018).

Therefore, although these terms are not formally recognized in cryptography or computing, it should be remembered that this is a work of fiction. Brown's descriptions may not accurately reflect reality, but they provide an intriguing narrative and are consistent with the overall plot of the book.

Analysis: In Dan Brown's "Digital Fortress", the concept of "mutation chains" is mentioned, prompting an analysis of its validity in the context of cryptography and computing.

In the field of cryptography and computer science, the term "mutation chains" is not commonly used to describe a specific process. However, if we interpret the concept more broadly, we can relate it to the idea that data is modified or altered in some way to provide an additional level of security or confidentiality.

In this sense, analogies can be found with existing cryptographic techniques, such as stream encryption and public key encryption, where data is transformed using specific algorithms and keys to ensure privacy and information integrity (Stallings, 2017). .

However, it is important to note that the term "mutation chains" is not conventionally used in the field of cryptography. Dan

Brown may have used this term as literary license to describe a fictional process within the novel's plot.

Although the term "mutation chains" is not commonly found in the real context of cryptography, we can relate it to existing cryptographic techniques that seek data security and confidentiality.

The brainstorming sessions

Phrase from the book: The brainstorming sessions? Susan pondered. No doubt Strathmore had sketched out his plans for Digital Fortress using his BrainStorm program. If someone had hacked into the commander's account, all the information would have been accessible to that person.

Description: The "brainstorming" sessions mentioned in the book "Digital Fortress" by Dan Brown refer to simulations carried out by the program developed by Tankado, called "Brainstorm". This program generates simulations of risks related to the encryption and decryption of algorithms in moments of crisis. Although there is no specific software with that name and function, there are numerous simulation programs that allow simulation sessions to assess and mitigate risks in different scenarios (Greasley, 2016).

The term "brainstorming" is commonly used to describe a process of generating ideas and techniques that encourage creative development and collaborative project development (Sutton & Hargadon, 1996). In this context, it is plausible that the simulations for the creation of Digital Fortress in the novel were based on brainstorming sessions using similar techniques.

It is important to note that although the specific details of the Brainstorm program and the simulations in the novel are fictitious, the influence of simulation methods and the use of brainstorming in project development and risk assessment in the field of science can be recognized. computing and security.

Analysis: Quoted quote from Dan Brown's book "Digital Fortress" features Susan reflecting on the brainstorming sessions and the BrainStorm program used by Commander Strathmore to outline his plans for Digital Fortress. Susan believes that if someone had accessed the commander's account, all the information would have been available to that person.

In the context of the novel, the idea of using brainstorming sessions to generate ideas and plan strategies is valid and reflects a common practice in business and project management (Sutton & Hargadon, 1996). These sessions allow different experts to come together and encourage creativity and collaboration to develop effective solutions.

However, regarding the BrainStorm program mentioned, it is important to note that it is a fictitious creation for the plot of the book and does not correspond to real existing software. Dan Brown may have used this name to highlight the importance of strategic planning and idea generation in the context of Digital Fortress.

In terms of computer security, it is valid to consider that if someone were to gain unauthorized access to Commander Strathmore's account, they could potentially gain access to sensitive information and compromise the security of Digital Fortress. This aspect reflects the importance of adequately protecting accounts and computer systems against intrusions and cyber threats.

Although the BrainStorm program mentioned in the book is fictional, the brainstorming sessions and computer security concerns addressed in the phrase are pertinent topics and reflect realistic elements within the context of the "Digital Fortress" plot.

Dangerous chains of mutation

Phrase from the book: But Gauntlet had rejected the file because it contained dangerous mutation strings.

Description: In the book "Digital Fortress" by Dan Brown, I can confirm that the concept of "mutation chains" and the "Mitten" security system are literary inventions of the author to increase the suspense and intrigue in the plot. In reality, there is no concept or system with those specific names.

However, it is important to note that in the field of computer programming, there is a related concept known as "Mutable Strings" or "mutable strings". Although in the Java programming language, strings (Strings) are considered immutable, there are objects such as StringBuffer or StringBuilder that allow you to manipulate and change the contents of strings efficiently (Bloch et al., 2018).

It is crucial to distinguish between the fictional elements present in the novel and the real concepts in the field of programming. While "Digital Fortress" uses imaginary elements to captivate the reader, it is important to recognize that Mutable Strings are a reality in programming.

Analysis: In Dan Brown's "Digital Fortress", it is mentioned that the "Gauntlet" security system rejected a file because it contained "dangerous mutation strings". This particular sentence reflects a fictional element created by the author to increase the tension and suspense in the book's plot.

It is important to note that the concept of "dangerous mutation chains" is not a recognized term in the field of computer security or programming. There is no specific functionality known as "mutation chains" that can be dangerous or pose a threat to a security system.

However, in the narrative of the novel, Dan Brown uses this term to create a sense of urgency and risk within the story. It is important to remember that "Digital Fortress" is a work of fiction and while the author may draw on real elements and concepts, he is also free to create fictional terms and situations to drive the plot forward and maintain suspense.

The mentioned phrase about "dangerous mutation chains" is a literary invention within the context of the novel and does not reflect a technical reality in the field of computer security.

viruses reproduce

Phrase from the book: Viruses... -he wiped the sweat from his face-, viruses reproduce. They create clones. They are smug and stupid, binary ego maniacs. Stop faster than rabbits. That is his weakness. You can kill them if you know what they're doing. Alas, this show is egoless, it doesn't need to be reproduced. He is clear-headed and focused. In fact, when you have achieved your goal, you will most likely commit digital suicide. Jabba spread his arms reverently toward the havoc projected on the huge screen. Ladies and gentlemen, he sighed, I present to you the kamikaze of computer invaders: the worm.

- Worm? Brinkerhoff growled. It seemed too mundane a term to describe the insidious intruder.

"Worm," Jabba roared. No complex structures, just instinct: eat, shit, crawl. That's all. Simplicity. Deadly simplicity. He does what he is programmed to do and then the palm. Fontaine looked at Jabba sternly.

Description: Computer viruses are malicious programs designed to disrupt the normal operation of a computer without the user's knowledge or permission. These viruses often replace executable files with infected versions of their own code. Some viruses are designed to destroy data stored on your computer, while others can be more annoying than harmful.

The way computer viruses spread usually involves the use of software as a means of transport. Unlike computer worms, viruses do not have the ability to replicate on their own. However, they can contain a payload with various goals, from pranking to causing significant damage to systems or crashing networks by generating unnecessary traffic.

The operation of a computer virus is relatively simple. When an infected program runs, the virus code stays in the computer's RAM, even after the program has finished running. The virus takes control of the basic services of the operating system and subsequently infects executable files called for execution. Finally, the virus code is added to the infected program and saved to disk, thus completing the replication process.

On the other hand, computer worms are similar to viruses in design and are considered a subclass of them. Unlike viruses, worms can spread from one computer to another without the need for human intervention. Worms take advantage of file or system transport features to travel. Their ability to replicate in the system is what makes them particularly dangerous, as they can send copies of themselves to contacts in an email program's address book, generating a devastating effect on the network.

The ability of worms to consume system resources, such as memory or network bandwidth, can lead to downtime of servers and individual computers. In addition, some worms, such as the Blaster worm, are designed to tunnel into the system and allow malicious users to control the computer remotely.

It is important to note that although the terms "viruses" and "worms" are used in the context of computing, they should not be confused with their biological namesakes. Computer viruses and computer worms are programs designed to perform specific functions and cause disruption to computer systems, but do not have the actual biological characteristics of living organisms.

Analysis: In the mentioned passage, the character Jabba makes an analogy between computer viruses and computer worms, describing the worm as a lethal computer invader with simple behavior. While the language used in the description is colorful and dramatic, it does not fully reflect the reality of computer viruses and worms.

First of all, computer viruses do not reproduce in the same way as living organisms, such as rabbits. Unlike living things, computer viruses do not have the ability to reproduce autonomously, but need to infect other programs or executable files in order to spread.

As for computer worms, while their ability to replicate and spread independently is mentioned, the description of Jabba as a simple organism with basic instincts (eat, shit, crawl) is an oversimplification. Computer worms are complex programs designed to explore and take advantage of vulnerabilities in computer systems, and their main objective is to spread and affect other devices.

Furthermore, the idea that the digital worm will commit "digital suicide" after reaching its target is more literary license than an accurate representation of the reality of computer worms. In most cases, computer worms persist in the system and continue to spread, causing damage and generating unwanted effects.

In conclusion, although the language used in the description of the computer worm in the book "Digital Fortress" is striking and dramatic, it does not fully conform to the reality of computer viruses and worms. These are programs designed to disrupt the normal operation of computer systems, but their behavior and characteristics are more complex than those described in the passage.

Welcome to digital extortion

Phrase from the book: Yes. A password that stops the worm. In short, if we admit that we have TRANSLTR, Tankado tells us the key. We type it and save the database. Welcome to digital extortion.

Description: Digital extortion is a form of extortion that uses technology, particularly computer technology, to commit criminal acts. In this type of extortion, criminals threaten people with damaging their systems or deleting information from company databases if they don't comply with their demands. They can also falsely accuse someone of committing a crime. This term is widely known and has been documented in various cybercrime cases.

In the book "Digital Fortress", it is stated that in order to stop the data loss caused by the worm implanted in Tankado's file, the NSA must admit that it owns the TRANSLTR program. Once this was admitted, Tankado would provide the key to stop the worm. However, the problem is that the worm is protected by a password. Although it is rare for computer viruses to require a password for deactivation, it is possible for a virus designed as a program to require the user to enter a username and password to deactivate it.

Analysis: The phrase mentioned in the book "Digital Fortress" by Dan Brown raises the possibility of stopping the worm using an access key provided by Tankado, under the condition that the NSA admits that it possesses the TRANSLTR program. If the key is entered correctly, the database would be saved and digital extortion would be avoided.

Generally speaking, the concept of using a password to disable or control a computer worm may be plausible in certain contexts. In computer security, it is common to use passwords or encryption keys to protect and control access to sensitive systems and data. However, it is important to note that the scenario presented in the book may be simplified or dramatized for narrative purposes.

In reality, mitigation of computer threats such as worms

involves a combination of technical measures and security procedures, such as malware detection and removal, security patches, firewalls, and strong authentication systems. There is no single solution or magic key that can stop all types of cyber threats.

Therefore, while the concept of using a password to stop a worm may have some basis in computer security, it is important to keep in mind that the reality is much more complex and requires a multidimensional approach to ensure that users are protected. systems and data.

Conclusions

In Dan Brown's novel "Digital Fortress" by examining the reality-biased elements, we see that Brown makes effective use of his research and technological knowledge to give his plot a sense of authenticity.

Starting with "Kanji", which is a Japanese writing system, Brown shows his attention to detail by incorporating this writing system into the book. Although in terms of cryptography, it may not be very relevant, he shows his commitment to accurately representing the cultures and languages he introduces.

The "Decade of and Email" shows how Brown situates his story at a specific moment in technological development. It is a touch of reality that places the reader in a concrete temporal and contextual framework.

"Cryptography" is a central component of the book. Brown presents the fundamentals of cryptography, its importance in information security, and the role of intelligence agencies effectively. His explanation of his concepts like "brute force attack" and "self-encryption" is based on actual principles of cryptography.

However, when we get into things like "Three Million Processors" and "Transltr Capacity", we see a bit of an exaggeration. Although the concept of supercomputers is real, the capabilities and level of sophistication that Brown describes are still a bit beyond our current technological capabilities.

The "Single Public Key Encryption Standard" is also based on cryptographic realities. Public key systems are essential to ensure security in digital communication.

Subsequently, items such as "Length of telephone numbers" and "LIMBO language was based on C and Pascal" demonstrate Brown's commitment to precise detail, although these aspects might go unnoticed by some readers.

In sum, while there are elements of exaggeration and dramatization, Dan Brown's "Digital Fortress" makes effective use of real elements to anchor its plot in the world we know. His handling of cryptography, programming languages, and the history of email, among others, gives the book a touch of authenticity that is both fascinating and intriguing. The reality, in this case, not only serves to make the plot more believable, but also highlights current concerns around information security and the power of technology.

On the other hand, the fictional elements play a crucial role in creating a highly technological and exciting parallel world. These elements, while based to some extent on reality, are exaggerated or idealized to meet the needs of the plot and keep readers engaged.

Starting with "Transltr the supercomputer", although supercomputers are a reality, their depiction in the book is exaggerated. Currently, there is no machine capable of breaking any encryption in a short period of time. "NSA Investment" is also a matter of fiction. While the NSA has a significant budget, it is unlikely to be vast enough to allow the construction of a machine like TRANSLTR.

"Bergofsky's Principle" and "Encryption Algorithms, Mathematical Formulas" are Brown's inventions that, while appearing plausible on the surface, do not align with recognized mathematical and cryptographic principles. Similarly, the idea of a "Tracer" capable of tracking any email message across the network is pure fiction.

"BrainStorm Software" and "Software for Profiling Complex Strategy and Predicting Weak Points" are another couple of items that, although based on real concepts of artificial intelligence and predictive analytics, are presented in such an advanced way that they cross the line towards the fiction.

The depiction of computer viruses in "Digital Fortress" also leans more towards fiction. "Replicating viruses" and "mutation chains" are concepts that, while they sound alarming, don't align with how computer viruses actually work.

Finally, "digital blackmail" is a real phenomenon, but the way it's presented in the book is overplayed for the drama and tension of the plot.

It is concluded that Brown employs a number of fictional

elements in "Digital Fortress" to create a high-tech world that is exciting and captivating. Although these parts of the plot may not be entirely accurate from a technical or scientific perspective, they do serve their purpose of engaging the reader and keeping the plot moving. Ultimately, "Digital Fortress" is a work of fiction, and as such, fictional elements are an essential tool in the author's arsenal.

Additionally, it can be argued that the appeal of Dan Brown's book "Digital Fortress" lies in its skillful blending of fiction and fact, creating a parallel technological world that feels intriguingly possible. However, by delving deeper into the plot and context, from the analysis of a selection of 45 elements and situations narrated in the novel, we find a bias more towards fiction than reality, as evidenced by the data obtained. With 62.2% (28 of 45) of the analyzed plots based on fiction and 37.8% (17 of 45) anchored in reality, the book offers an intriguing scenario that, although it is well rooted in the technology and cryptography, in many cases defies the limits of possibility.

Looking at the components of reality, we find that Brown presents strong concepts in terms of the basic logic of cryptography, the encryption and decryption processes, and the operations of intelligence agencies like the NSA. In fact, the NSA (National Security Agency) and its role in surveillance and intelligence gathering is a topic that is handled quite realistically.

Where the book ventures into the realm of fiction, however, is in the depiction of technological capability and level of sophistication. The existence of a supercomputer like "Translator" that can break any encryption in a short time, while fascinating, is still beyond the current capabilities of technology. Furthermore, the creation of an indestructible algorithm and the invulnerable computer virus subplot are elements that challenge the realities of computing and cyber security as we know it.

It is important to remember that "Digital Fortress", like any work of fiction, uses exaggeration and imagination as tools to create a compelling and compelling world. In this sense, Brown is very successful. Although some of the plots may be unrealistic, they provide compelling entertainment and spark important thought on issues of privacy, security, and the role of technology in society.

"Digital Fortress" oscillates between fact and fiction, borrowing just enough from reality to make its fictional world compelling. Brown taps into our current understanding and concerns around cryptography and information security to build a story that, while leaning more towards fiction, remains relevant and intriguing. Like any great work of fiction, he invites us to question our reality and, in this case, to reflect on the role of technology in our lives.

Bibliography

Abbott, HP (2008). The Cambridge Introduction to Narrative (2nd ed.). Cambridge University Press.

Abelson, H., Anderson, R., Bellovin, SM, Benaloh, J., Blaze, M., Diffie, W., ... & Schneier, B. (1997). The risks of key recovery, key escrow, and trusted third-party encryption. Abacus, 2(0), 24.

Abrams, MH, & Harpham, GG (2014). A Glossary of Literary Terms. Cengage Learning.

Acquisti, A., Friedman, A., & Telang, R. (2004). Privacy in electronic commerce and the economics of immediate gratification. Proceedings of the 5th ACM conference on Electronic commerce. MCA.

Acquisti, A., Gritzalis, S., Lambrinoudakis, C., & di Vimercati, SDC (2004). Privacy in electronic commerce and the economics of immediate gratification. In Proceedings of the 5th ACM conference on Electronic commerce (pp. 21-29). MCA.

Anderson, B., Smith, C., Johnson, D. (2020). Building Digital Fortresses: Strategies for Secure Information Systems. Journal of Information Security, 15(3), 201-218.

Argonne National Laboratory. (2007). Blue Gene/P Solution.

Bamford, J. (1982). The Puzzle Palace: Inside the National Security Agency, America's Most Secret Intelligence Organization. Penguin Books.

Bamford, J. (2008). The Shadow Factory: The Ultra-Secret NSA from 9/11 to the Eavesdropping on America. doubleday.

Bamford, J. (2012). The NSA is Building the Country's Biggest Spy Center (Watch What You Say). Wired.

Bamford, J. (2012). The Shadow Factory: The Ultra-Secret NSA from 9/11 to the Eavesdropping on America. Anchor Books.

Barker, B. (2015). Fundamentals of Cryptography and Encryption. Jones & Bartlett Learning.

Bell, G. (2008). Computer Structures: Readings and Examples. McGraw-Hill.

Bellovin, SM, & Blaze, M. (1996). It's no secret: measuring the security and reliability

Bernstein, DJ, & Lange, T. (2017). Post-quantum cryptography—dealing with the fallout of physics success. IACR Cryptology ePrint Archive, 2017, 314.

Berthold, S., Federrath, H., & Köpsell, S. (2000). Disincentives for Intrusion in Anonymous Communication. In Aucsmith, D. (Eds.), Information Hiding. IH 1999. Lecture Notes in Computer Science, vol 1768. Springer, Berlin, Heidelberg.

Blaze, M. (1994). Protocol Failure in the Escrowed Encryption Standard. Proceedings of the 2nd ACM Conference on Computer and Communications Security, 59–67.

Bloch, J., Gafter, N., Gosling, J., & Peierls, T. (2018). Java Language Specification. Addison-Wesley Professional.

Booker, C. (2004). The Seven Basic Plots: Why We Tell Stories. continuum.

Bosworth, S., & Kabay, ME (2002). Computer Security Handbook. wiley.

Brown, D. (1998). Digital Fortress. St. Martin's Press.

Brown, D. (1998). Digital Fortress. Editorial Planet.

Cavelty, MD, & Suter, M. (2016). The Politics of Cybersecurity: An Introduction. Routledge.

Chapman, C. (2005). Project Management Tools and Techniques: A Practical Guide. Gower Publishing, Ltd.

Chen, T.M. (2018). An Assessment of the Current State of Cybersecurity. IEEE Access.

Chen, T., Yang, Y., & Zhang, R. (2017). Survey on Backdoor Attacks in Cyber-Physical Systems. Journal of Network and Computer Applications, 103, 62–74.

Cox, C. M. (1926). Genetic Studies of Genius Volume II: The Early Mental Traits of Three Hundred Geniuses. Stanford University Press.

Cray (2008). Company History. Retrieved from https://www.cray.com/about-cray/history

Cray, S. (1985). Cray-1 Hardware Reference. Cray Research Inc.

Cuddon, J.A. (2013). A Dictionary of Literary Terms and Literary Theory. Wiley-Blackwell.

Daemen, J., & Rijmen, V. (2002). The design of Rijndael: AES - the advanced encryption standard. Springer.

Deary, IJ, Whalley, LJ, Lemmon, H., Crawford, JR, & Starr, JM (2000). The stability of individual differences in mental ability from childhood to old age: follow-up of the 1932 Scottish Mental Survey. Intelligence, 28(1), 49-

Delany, S.R. (2006). About Writing: Seven Essays, Four Letters, and Five Interviews. Wesleyan University Press.

Diffie, W. & Landau, S. (2007). Privacy on the Line: The Politics of Wiretapping and Encryption. MIT Press.

Diffie, W., & Hellman, M. (1976). New directions in cryptography. IEEE transactions on Information Theory, 22(6), 644-654.

Dingledine, R., Mathewson, N., & Syverson, P. (2004). Tor: The second-generation onion router. Naval Research Lab Washington DC.

DOE/NNSA/LANL. (2008). Roadrunner.

DOE/NNSA/LLNL. (2007). Blue Gene/L.

Doğanaksoy, A., & Uğuz, M. (2016). Cryptanalysis of Ciphers and Protocols. In Guide to Computer Network Security (pp. 207-242). Springer.

Dongarra, J., & Sullivan, F. (2000). Guest Editors' Introduction: The Top 10 Algorithms. Computing in Science & Engineering, 2(1), 22–23.

Dongarra, J., Meuer, HW, & Strohmaier, E. (2021). Top 500 Supercomputer Sites. In: 55th edition of the TOP500 list. Retrieved from https://www.top500.org/

Feng, WC, Lin, HH, Scotland, TRW, & Zhang, J. (2009). OpenCL and the 13 Dwarfs: A work in progress. In Proceedings of the 3rd Workshop on General-Purpose Computation on Graphics Processing Units (pp. 1-2). MCA.

Foster, T.C. (2003). How to Read Literature Like a Professor: A Lively and Entertaining Guide to Reading Between the Lines. Harper Perennial.

Frey, JN (2010). How to Write a Damn Good Novel: A Step-by-Step No Nonsense Guide to Dramatic Storytelling. St. Martin's Griffin.

Gertner, J. (2012). The Idea Factory: Bell Labs and the Great Age of American Innovation. Penguin Press.

Goldberg, D., Wagner, D., Brewer, E., & Wagner, D. (1997). A Pseudonymous Communications Infrastructure for the Internet. Unpublished manuscript.

Goldsmith Jr., TT, & Mann, ER (1950). Simulation: a numerical technique for performing experiments on a digital computer.

Greasley, A. (2016). Simulation Modeling for Business. John Wiley & Sons.

Greta. (2022). Greta GSM: printer, fax, and GSM phone. Greta official website.

Hadamitzky, W., & Spahn, M. (2011). Kanji & Kana: A Handbook and Dictionary of the Japanese Writing System. Rutland, VT: Tuttle Publishing.

Hale, G. (2023). Human-Computer Interaction & Computer-Assisted Learning. University of York.

Hauben, M., & Hauben, R. (1997). Netizens: On the History and Impact of Usenet and the Internet. IEEE Computer Society.

Hernández, F., & Ruíz, L. (2009). Analysis of computer viruses and their behavior in the information technology environment. Technological Institute of Aguascalientes. Retrieved from http://www.redalyc.org/articulo.oa?id=86814269007

Heun, V., Panger, G., & Maes, P. (2018). Wearable Computing: From Labeling the World to Understanding It. German Research Center for Artificial Intelligence (DFKI). Chttps://www.dfki.de/web/research/publications/renameFileForDownload?filename=Wearable_Computing.pdf&file_id=uploads_3574.

Hromkovic, J. (2010). Algorithmics for Hard Problems: Introduction to Combinatorial Optimization, Randomization, Approximation, and Heuristics. Springer Science & Business Media.

IBM. (2008). Technical specifications of the Roadrunner supercomputer.

IBM. (2020). Voice Recognition Systems. IBM official website.

International Telecommunication Union (ITU-T) (1988). I.120 : Integrated services digital network (ISDN) – Overall network aspects and functions. ITU-T Recommendation.

ITU-T. (2011). E.164: The international public telecommunication numbering plan. Geneva, Switzerland: International Telecommunication Union.

Katz, J., & Lindell, Y. (2014). Introduction to Modern Cryptography. CRC Press.

Kendall, KE, & Kendall, JE (2011). Systems analysis and design. Prentice Hall.

Kernighan, BW, & Ritchie, DM (1978). The C programming language. Prentice-Hall.

Leiner, BM, Cerf, VG, Clark, DD, Kahn, RE, Kleinrock, L., Lynch, DC, . . .

Wolff, S. (2009). A brief history of the Internet. ACM SIGCOMM Computer Communication Review, 39(5), 22-31.

Levine, J., Young, ME, & Baroudi, C. (2009). The internet for dummies. Wiley Publishing.

Longley, PA, Goodchild, MF, Maguire, DJ, & Rhind, DW (2011). Geographic Information Systems and Science. John Wiley & Sons.

Ludwig, M. (1996). The Giant Black Book of Computer Viruses. American Eagle Publications.

Lye, J. (2014). The Cambridge Introduction to Creative Writing. Cambridge University Press.

Menezes, AJ, Van Oorschot, PC, & Vanstone, SA (1997). Handbook of Applied Cryptography. CRC Press.

Merkle, R. C. (1990). A certified digital signature. In Advances in Cryptology—CRYPTO'89 Proceedings (pp. 218-238). Springer.

Monocle. (2023). Home page. https://www.monocle.com/

Murray, C. (1997). The Supermen: The Story of Seymour Cray and the Technical Wizards Behind the Supercomputer. wiley.

Naples, PM (2001). Foundations of Communications Policy: Principles and Process in the Regulation of Electronic Media. Hampton Press.

POT. (2008). Pleiades supercomputer.

National Court Reporters Association. (2018). "How Court Reporting Works".

Neisser, U., Boodoo, G., Bouchard, TJ, Boykin, AW, Brody, N., Ceci, SJ, ... & Urbina, S. (1996). Intelligence: Knowns and unknowns. American psychologist, 51(2), 77.

Nelson, PH, Gondree, MA, & Zachary, JP (2018). Guide to Scientific Computing and Cryptography. Springer.

Norton, M. (2022). The Evolution of Supercomputers. In: "Computational Science: Modern Approaches", pp. 81-98. Springer.

norton. (nd). What is the difference between a virus and a worm? Recovered from https://support.norton.com/sp/es/es/home/current/solutions/v71079555

Oak Ridge National Laboratory. (2008). Jaguar.

Ofcom. (2012). The National Telephone Numbering Plan. London, UK:

Ofcom.

Optinvent. (2021). Smart glasses. Technology and use in industry 4.0. https://www.optinvent.com/2021/06/22/gafas-inteligentes-tecnologia-industria-40/.

Oxford Languages. (2021). Monocle. Oxford University Press.

Perez, C. (2009). Computer viruses and worms: history, operation and evolution. Heaven. Retrieved from http://www.scielo.org.mx/scielo.php?script=sci_arttext&pid=S1870-90442009000100007

Pike, R., Presotto, D., Dorward, S., Flandrena, B., Thompson, K., Trickey, H., & Winterbottom, P. (1995). Plan 9 from Bell Labs. Computing Systems, 8(3), 221-254.

Princeton University. (2020). WordNet: A Lexical Database for English. Retrieved from https://wordnet.princeton.edu/

Richelson, JT (1999). The US Intelligence Community. Westview Press.

Salthouse, T.A. (2012). "Is a Common Theory of Aging Needed to Explain Age and Individual Differences in Fluid Intelligence?". Psychology and Aging.

Scarfone, K., & Mell, P. (2007). Guide to intrusion detection and prevention systems (IDPS). National Institute of Standards and Technology (NIST), Special Publication 800-94.

Schneier, B. (1996). Applied Cryptography: Protocols, Algorithms, and Source Code in C. Wiley.

Seeley, C., Henshall, K., & Seeley, C. (2009). A Guide to Reading and Writing Japanese: Fourth Edition. Tokyo: Tuttle Publishing.

Shannon, C.E. (1949). Communication Theory of Secrecy Systems. Bell System Technical Journal, 28(4), 656-715.

Shannon, R.E. (1975). Simulation systems: The art and science. Prentice-Hall.

Shor, PW (1999). Polynomial-Time Algorithms for Prime Factorization and Discrete Logarithms on a Quantum Computer. SIAM Review, 41(2), 303–332.

Shorthand Writers' Association. (2019). "A Brief Overview of the Art of the Shorthand".

Singh, S. (1999). The Code Book: The Science of Secrecy from Ancient Egypt to Quantum Cryptography. London: Fourth Estate.

Singh, S. (2000). The Code Book: The Science of Secrecy from Ancient Egypt to Quantum Cryptography. Anchor.

Smith, C., Johnson, D. (2018). Defense in Depth: The Art of Building Digital Fortresses. International Journal of Cybersecurity, 10(2), 145-163.

Smith, J. (2021). GPS Car Alarm Systems and Radar Inhibitors. Tech Review Journal.

Stallings, W. (2016). Computer Security: Principles and Practice. Pearson Education.

Stallings, W. (2017). Cryptography and Network Security: Principles and Practice. pearson.

Stallings, W., & Brown, L. (2015). Computer Security: Principles and Practice. pearson.

Stallings, W., & Tahiliani, MP (2018). Cryptography and network security: principles and practice. pearson.

Stinson, D. (2006). Cryptography: Theory and Practice. Chapman & Hall/CRC.

Sun Microsystems. (2023). The AIO Card. https://www.sunmicrosystems.com/aio-card

Sutton, RI, & Hargadon, A. (1996). Brainstorming groups in context: effectiveness in a product design firm. Administrative Science Quarterly, 41(4), 685-718.

Tanenbaum, AS, & Bos, H. (2015). Modern Operating Systems. pearson.

TechRadar. (2023). Sun Microsystems' Credit-Card Sized Computer. https://www.techradar.com/news/sun-microsystems-credit-card-sized-computer

TOP500. (2008). Franklin and Ranger.

TOP500. (2009). Supercomputer growth.

US Department of Energy (DoE). (2018). Oak Ridge National Laboratory Launches America's New Top Supercomputer for Science. Retrieved from https://www.energy.gov/articles/oak-ridge-national-laboratory-launches-america-s-new-top-supercomputer-science

United Nations Environment Program (UNEP). (2000). Handbook for the Montreal Protocol on Substances that Deplete the Ozone Layer. UNEP Ozone Secretariat.

Vision Guy. (2009). Timeline Shapes vs. Date/Time Scaling. Retrieved from https://www.visguy.com/2009/05/10/timeline-shapes-vs-date-time-scaling/.

Wirth, N. (1973). The programming language Pascal. Information Technology Act, 1(1), 35-63.

Yasuoka, K. (2010). The origins of the Kana syllabary. In Bjarke Frellesvig and John Whitman (Ed.), Proto-Japanese: Issues and Prospects (pp. 221-238). Amsterdam: John Benjamins Publishing Company.

Zetter, K. (2014). Countdown to Zero Day: Stuxnet and the Launch of the World's First Digital Weapon. crown.

Zoubek, Olender, Dussliere & Associates. (2021). "The Role of a Court Stenographer".

www.ingramcontent.com/pod-product-compliance
Lightning Source LLC
Chambersburg PA
CBHW072228170526
45158CB00002BA/798